599

Katona, Steven

A Field guide to the whales
and seals of the Gulf of Maine

DATE DUE

SEP 2 8 2005	

D1261277

2.15

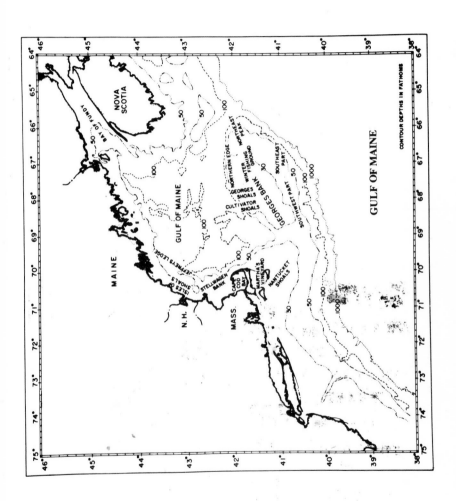

A Field Guide
to the
Whales and Seals
of the
Gulf of Maine

Text by
Steven Katona · David Richardson
Robin Hazard

Illustrations by
John Quinn · D.D. Tyler

Copyright © 1975
by Steven Katona, David Richardson

Library of Congress Catalog Card Number: 75-18920
International Standard Book Number: 0-916080-01-3

Illustrated by John Quinn and D.D. Tyler.
Designed by D.D. Tyler.
Printed by Maine Coast Printers, Rockland, Maine.

Front cover, right whale, by John Quinn.
Back cover, nursing harbor seal, by D.D. Tyler.

CONTENTS

right whale
(page 23)

PREFACE

At least 21 species of whales and porpoises, plus 5 species of seals have been recorded within the area between the north shore of Cape Cod, Cape Sable, Nova Scotia and the shallow fishing banks which run between them. That area is called the Gulf of Maine, and this field guide has been designed for use by the interested mariner, fisherman, or visitor who wants to learn to identify the whales and seals which swim there.

The guide includes drawings and basic information on every whale or seal species which has been identified in the Gulf of Maine, whether it has been seen once or thousands of times, alive at sea, or dead on a beach. Part 1 is devoted to the whales, Part 2 to the seals. Each part contains introductory comments, a summary of information on distribution, habitat and abundance of the species, and a short description plus one or more illustrations of each species. Every effort has been made to present this information as simply as possible. Suggestions for further reading can be found at the end of each part so that interested readers can explore topics in more depth.

Both the text and the illustrations emphasize the importance of field marks for species identification. Field marks are outstanding color patterns, body shapes or behavior traits which can be used by observers to distinguish particular species rapidly and accurately in the wild. As in birdwatching, it pays to know field marks of the various species well, because different whales or seals are frequently difficult to tell apart, and because often only a small part of the animal can be seen and only for a second or two. Since most whales or seals will be seen from a distance, good binoculars (7 power x 35 or 50 mm) will usually be necessary. Instruments with greater magnification can be used on land, but are hard to hold on a rocking boat. Similarly, telephoto lenses longer than about 200 mm for a 35 mm camera will require a combination of fast film speed, a chest mount or rifle mount and a very steady hand when used from a boat. The text describes several locations where these animals can sometimes be observed from land with a telescope. Finally, a good measure of patience and luck will often be necessary for successful whale or seal watching.

Watching whales or seals can provide observers with a unique and exhilarating natural experience. Equally important, accurate written reports or photographs of your experiences can be a valuable addition to the available information on these animals, which are still very poorly understood. We would be grateful to receive accounts of all sightings of injured, dead, or unusual seals or of living or dead whales or porpoises from the New England region. Sample sighting report forms are provided in this guide. A great deal can be learned from even a dead animal, and all information obtained will be forwarded to the Marine Mammal Salvage Program of the Smithsonian Institution, in Washington, D.C. Stranded animals, living or dead, should be reported immediately to the local police, coastal warden, or National Marine Fisheries Service in Portland, Maine (207-775-3131) or Gloucester, Massachusetts (617-283-8802).

At this point, we wish to acknowledge the people whose help made this first edition of the field guide possible. We are especially grateful to William A. Watkins (Woods Hole Oceanographic Institution), William E. Schevill (Harvard University and Woods Hole Oceanographic Institution), Dr. Dale Rex Coman, Dr. David E. Sergeant (Fisheries Research Board of Canada) and Dr. William H. Drury (Massachusetts Audubon Society) for critical readings of portions of the manuscript and for many constructive suggestions. We also owe a special debt of thanks to Dr. Edward D. Mitchell (Fisheries Research Board of Canada) for sharing his hard-won whale watching experiences with us during discussions or seminars. Additional comments from Dr. Roger Payne, Katy Payne, Scott Kraus, Steve Savage, Gayle Cliett, Sydney Rathbun and Kate Darling have been helpful. Finally, we wish to thank the National Science Foundation

(GY 11454), The National Geographic Society, and the Massachusetts and National Audubon Societies for supporting portions of the research which led up to this project.

Despite all the help we have been given, some mistakes will undoubtedly be found in the guide. We will welcome any further suggestions as to how it could be made more accurate, easier to use, or more comprehensive.

Steven K. Katona
College of the Atlantic
Bar Harbor, Maine 04609
1-207-288-5015

David Richardson
Fisheries Research Station
Maine Department of Marine Resources
West Boothbay Harbor, Maine 04575
1-207-633-5572

mother and calf finback whales, Mt. Desert Rock, Maine, August 1975

Part 1.
WHALES, DOLPHINS AND PORPOISES

INTRODUCTION

Through the ages, whales and people have been involved together in myth, literature, art, music and commerce. In general, people tended to be mainly interested in products that could be made from whales, although some early scientists tried to learn about the whales themselves. As the apparently high intelligence and trainability of some porpoises (which are really only little whales) became recognized during the past 20 years, public interest in the biology of whales in general increased. Recordings of the remarkable sounds of humpback whales and killer whales, as well as many recent films and articles on whales, have further stimulated public interest. Now, when a number of whales are already on the endangered species list, it is clear how little we really know about these creatures, whose unusual adaptations for life in the water make them some of the most interesting of all mammals.

All of the whales, dolphins and porpoises belong to the group of mammals called cetaceans. Like all other mammals, they breathe air with lungs, have warm blood, bear live young and suckle them with milk from mammary glands. However, they differ from all other mammals because they have no fur, except for a few hairs on the head in some species, and they have no hind legs. The examination of living and fossil cetaceans suggests that they descended from land mammals, perhaps beginning about 50 million years ago. Over the millenia, the tail evolved into the major organ of locomotion. Wide flukes made of cartilage developed on the sides of the tail for propulsion and steering. All that remains of the hind limbs is a pair of small bones representing the pelvis, located about where the rear limbs of a land mammal would connect with the backbone. The forelimbs evolved into flippers at the sides of the whale, used mainly as stabilizers or for steering. Most whales also have a dorsal fin on the back, which may help them to maintain a steady course without rolling from side to side.

Underneath the smooth skin is a layer of fat called blubber, which stores food energy, helps to insulate the animal in cold water, and contributes to its even, streamlined form. The blubber may be only about an inch thick in porpoises, which are usually less than ten feet long and weigh several hundred pounds, but it may be up to two feet thick in some of the larger whales, which may approach 100 feet in length and 200,000 pounds. Blubber was boiled down in times past to make oil for burning in lamps and for lubrication.

The mechanism for breathing has also been modified during cetacean evolution. The nostrils, found at the snout tip in all other mammals, are located on the top of the head in nearly all species. As a result, a whale can continue swimming as it breathes through this "blowhole," because only the very top of the head must break the water surface. Cetaceans also empty and fill their lungs much more completely and quickly than do other mammals, thus minimizing the time spent at the surface. High concentrations of respiratory pigments in the blood and muscle bind large amounts of oxygen to maximize the amount of time that the animals can stay underwater. At the surface, a whale's exhaled breath is often visible as a spout, which is probably the result of condensation of the warm, moist, slightly-compressed air from the lungs as it encounters cold sea air. It is possible that the spout also contains either water or mucus that is being cleared out of the breathing passage. Many cetaceans, especially the porpoises or dolphins, do not always show a spout when they exhale, and are therefore harder to spot at sea.

Cetaceans are divided into two major suborders, the *odontoceti* (from the Greek *odontos*, teeth, and *ketos*, a whale) and the *mysticeti* (from the Greek *mystax*, a moustache).

The sketches shown below of cetaceans from the two groups will help to familiarize readers with their shapes and the locations of external body parts.

Odontocetes, or toothed cetaceans, with the exception of the sperm whale, are relatively small, usually well under 30 feet in length. They generally pursue individual prey, such as squid, fish, and very rarely birds or mammals. Some species have been shown to use echolocation to find food, and many other species are suspected to have that ability. Nearly 90 species of toothed cetaceans are known to exist, and perhaps a few more will be discovered as we learn more about the oceans. Many of the smaller types are known as porpoises or dolphins. It has often been said that porpoises have a blunt head and flattened, spade-shaped teeth, whereas dolphins have jaws which are drawn out into a long snout and which contain pointed teeth. In fact, examination of skulls reveals that the jaws are drawn out as a long

GENERALIZED WHALE TYPES

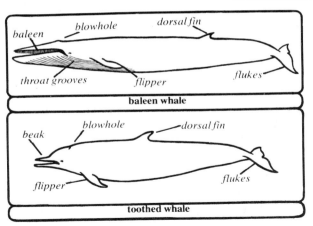

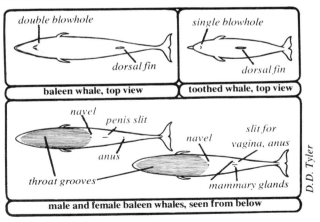

snout (sometimes called a beak) in all dolphins or porpoises. However, various species differ in the amount of tissue filling the space between the front of the skull and the top of the extended jaws. When there is little tissue, the protruding jaws are clearly visible externally as a beak. However, in species with a large amount of this tissue, the elongation of the jaws is hidden. In such species, this tissue is called the melon, because it is rounded and has a firm, pulpy, fibrous appearance when sliced open. In the pothead and northern bottlenosed whale, for example, the melon sometimes bulges out over the tip of the jaws. Experiments have shown that some porpoises use this dense tissue as an acoustic lens, varying its shape to focus sound pulses. Since external beaks are visible in some porpoises and are lacking in some dolphins, it is best to consider the two names to be interchangeable. Most sailors call these animals porpoises. Use of that word alone would eliminate confusion with the warm-water fish *Coryphaena hippurus*, whose common name is dolphin.

Mysticetes have no teeth, but instead possess a series of horny plates, called baleen or "whalebone," which hang down from the roof of the mouth and whose frayed inner edges are used to filter plankton from the water for food. These whales are first seen as fossils from about 30 million years ago and probably evolved from toothed ancestors. The mysticete whales related to the blue whale all

BALEEN

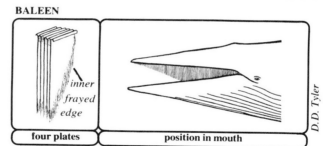

inner frayed edge

four plates

position in mouth

D.D. Tyler

have a number of folds or grooves on the throat and chest. When cut in cross-section, the ridge between each two grooves looks like a tube. Whalers therefore named such whales "rorquals" from the Norwegian words *ror*, tube, and *hval*, whale. The approximate maximum number of grooves in the blue, finback, sei and minke whales is respectively, 90, 80, 60 and 50. In sei and minke whales, the grooves do not extend much beyond the flippers, but in the other three species they reach the navel. The humpback whale is in a different genus, but it has up to about 25 wide grooves which extend to the navel, and it is a modified rorqual whale. The right whale and its relatives have no grooves at all, and the gray whale, which is now found only on our Pacific coast, has only two grooves. When the whale gulps a mouthful of water containing food, the grooves stretch, allowing the floor of the mouth to balloon outwards so that the largest possible volume of water can be entrapped. Recent evidence suggests the possibility that mysticete whales may produce sounds which could be used for echolocation of food; however, this possibility has not been tested by experiments.

No estimates of past or present population sizes are yet available for whales in the Gulf of Maine. The American whaling industry began in New England in the mid-1600's, but soon most of the hunting took place in distant waters. However, early whalers working from shore stations hunted humpback whales and right whales from Cape Cod and other parts of Massachusetts during the 1600's and early 1700's. Porpoises and pilot whales were also hunted or driven ashore during those years. By 1750 right whales were very rare in the Gulf of Maine, and they remain so today. During the next century, coastal whaling for humpbacks and finbacks was carried out along the Maine coast from such ports as Winter Harbor, Prospect Harbor and Tremont; however, catches were not large. For example, an average of 6 to 7 whales, mostly finbacks, was taken annually from Prospect Harbor during 1835-1840, the peak whaling years in that area. Some hunting was also done in Cape Cod and Massachusetts Bays during the 1800's. Micmac Indians in the Bay of Fundy region hunted porpoises for oil in the late 1800's. It is possible that coastal whaling from stations south of Cape Cod affected the numbers of whales reaching the Gulf of Maine during the eighteenth and nineteenth centuries. Little hunting took place after 1900. Canadian whaling stations in Nova Scotia and Newfoundland operated during the past 100 years, and may possibly have taken some whales which would have spent time in the Gulf of Maine. The Canadian whaling stations suspended their activities in 1972 and most whale populations which reach the Gulf of Maine probably are not now hunted in any parts of their ranges. The hunting, harrassing and killing of marine mammals is now strictly prohibited to U.S. citizens by the Marine Mammal Protection Act of 1972. Whether this will be sufficient to increase their numbers remains to be seen.

Of the 100 or so species of cetaceans known to exist, 21 have been identified, either dead or living, in the Gulf of Maine. Of these, five are seen often; one was common in historical times but is now rare; and four are seen occasionally. The remaining 11 species include some types which are rare here, but common in other regions, as well as some which appear to be rare everywhere. Within the body of this field guide, the species have been arranged for the convenience of the observer, with baleen whales first, followed by toothed whales. Within each group, the more commonly seen species are described first.

Although the locations of whales cannot be predicted as easily as the locations of seals, several places along our coast may provide good whalewatching. Whales and porpoises can often be seen from land during summer at Head Harbor Light on Campobello Island, N.B., Canada; and West Quoddy Head near Lubec, Maine. Harbor porpoises can often be seen from near the Bass Harbor Light, on Mt. Desert Island. During April or May, dolphins and occasional whales can be seen from the dunes on Cape Cod, especially near Wellfleet or at Race Point. Ferryboats which cross the Gulf of Maine, such as the *MV Bluenose* (Bar Harbor-Yarmouth, N.S.) or *MV Bolero* and *MV Prince of Fundy* (Portland-Yarmouth, N.S.) provide an excellent opportunity for whalewatching. Fishing banks are good locations for spotting whales or porpoises, especially when schools of young fish are abundant. Whales are spotted with some regularity near Grand Manan Island, New Brunswick; and Mount Desert Rock and Matinicus Rock, Maine, during July, August and September. Stellwagen Bank, Jeffreys

Ledge and other more southerly areas in the Gulf of Maine appear to have whales earlier in the spring and later in the autumn than do the more northerly areas. When whalewatching, be alert for groups of diving birds, which signal the presence of fish or plankton, because whales may often be seen feeding in the same area. Your sighting reports will help us to make better predictions of where and when whales can be seen most easily.

SUMMARY OF OCCURRENCE OF WHALES OF THE GULF OF MAINE

Family / *Species* / Common Name	Western North Atlantic Range and Distribution	Habitat	Estimated Abundance in Western North Atlantic	Relative Dominance in Gulf of Maine
Common:				
Phocoenidae / *Phocoena phocoena* / Harbor porpoise	New Jersey to Baffin Bay. Center of population in approaches to Bay of Fundy and inshore Gulf of Maine	Coastal and inshore waters	Not known	Numerically dominant cetacean
Delphinidae / *Globicephala melaena* / Pothead, Pilot whale	New York to Greenland. Especially common in Newfoundland	Pelagic (winter) and coastal (summer)	No estimates. Most common whale seen in Cape Cod Bay. Schools of up to 300 on Georges Bank	Frequently seen

Name	Range	Habitat	Abundance	Dominance
Balaenopteridae *Balaenoptera physalus* Finback whale	Equator to pack ice. Population centered between 41°21′N and 57°00′N and from coast to 200 m contour	Pelagic, but enters bays and inshore waters in late summer	7,200	Dominant large whale; one of most common cetaceans
Balaenopteridae *Balaenoptera acutorostrata* Minke whale	Chesapeake Bay to Baffin Island in summer; eastern Gulf of Mexico, northeast Florida and Bahamas in winter	Pelagic, but may come closer to shore than do other rorquals (except humpback)	Less than 46,000	Reported less often than finback, but sightings are routine
Balaenopteridae *Megaptera novaeangliae* Humpback whale	Caribbean Sea to Arctic	Pelagic, but breeds in shallow water near warm-water islands and comes close to land during migrations and feeding	1,200	Routinely seen, but may be reduced from past abundance

Name	Range	Habitat	Abundance	Dominance
Historically Common:				
Balaenidae *Eubalaena glacialis* Right whale	New England to Davis Straits and Newfoundland. Occasionally as far south as Florida	Pelagic and coastal. Sometimes comes inshore	Several hundred	Much reduced from former importance. Not common now
Occasional:				
Delphinidae *Lagenorhynchus acutus* White-sided dolphin	Cape Cod to Davis Strait. Occasionally seen in Gulf of Maine	Pelagic or coastal. Sometimes schools with potheads	No estimate	Usually not important by numbers, but large schools may appear occasionally
Delphinidae *Lagenorhynchus albirostris* White-beaked dolphin	Massachusetts to Davis Strait, but ranges farther north than *L. acutus*. Not common south of Labrador or Newfoundland	Offshore or coastal	No estimate	Apparently minimal

Name	Range	Habitat	Abundance	Dominance
Delphinidae *Delphinis delphis* Saddleback dolphin	Jamaica to New-foundland. Widely distributed. May be most abundant dolphin in world	Seldom found inside 100 m contour, but does frequent seamounts and other offshore features	No estimate. Probably more common than available records indicate	Not known. Possibly *Phocoena* is a competitor
Delphinidae *Orcinus orca* Killer whale	Bahamas to Arctic. Rare in Gulf of Maine	Mainly pelagic and oceanic, however does approach coast	No estimate. Apparently not seen as commonly as in more northerly areas	May be somewhat more common than reports would suggest
Rare:				
Delphinidae *Tursiops truncatus* Bottlenose dolphin	Tropics to Greenland, but most common from Florida, West Indies, and Caribbean to New England	Usually close to shore and near islands. Enters bays, lagoons, rivers	No estimate	Rare. Perhaps *Phocoena* is a competitor

Name	Range	Habitat	Abundance	Dominance
Delphinidae *Grampus griseus* Gray grampus	South from Massachusetts. Range poorly known	Warm offshore waters. Habitat poorly known	No estimate	Poorly known. Apparently of minimal importance
Delphinidae *Stenella coeruleoalba* Striped dolphin	Caribbean to Greenland	Pelagic in tropical and warm waters	No estimate	Minimal
Monodontidae *Delphinapteras leucas* Beluga	St. Lawrence River and Gulf to Arctic. Rarely as far south as Long Island Sound	Prefers estuaries and shallow waters	1,000 in Gulf of St. Lawrence. No other estimate	Rare
Balaenopteridae *Balaenoptera borealis* Sei whale	Mexico to Arctic	Pelagic, does not usually approach coast	1,570 off Nova Scotia	Poorly known

Name	Range	Habitat	Abundance	Dominance
Balaenopteridae *Balaenoptera musculus* Blue whale	From about 35°N toward pole	Pelagic, deep ocean. Occasionally near land in deep-water areas, such as St. Lawrence River	Several hundred. Pre-whaling population estimated at 1,100	Minimal
Physeteridae *Physeter catodon* Sperm whale	Equator to 50°N (females & juveniles) or Davis Strait (males)	Pelagic, deep ocean	Estimate 22,000 inhabit North Atlantic Ocean	Rare visitor. May be more important on offshore banks
Physeteridae *Kogia breviceps* Pygmy sperm whale	Florida and Texas to Nova Scotia	Pelagic in warm ocean waters	No estimates. Usually considered rare	Minimal
Ziphiidae *Hyperoodon ampullatus* Northern bottlenose whale	Rhode Island to Davis Strait	Pelagic in cold temperate and sub-arctic deep water	Poorly known. Between 260-270 taken annually in North Atlantic Ocean, 1968-1970	Minimal

Name	Range	Habitat	Abundance	Dominance
Ziphiidae *Mesoplodon mirus* True's beaked whale	Northern Florida to Nova Scotia	Poorly known	Extremely rare. No estimate	Minimal
Ziphiidae *Mesoplodon densirostris* Dense-beaked whale	Bahamas to Nova Scotia	Probably pelagic in tropical and warm waters	Extremely rare. No estimate	Minimal

John Quinn

FINBACK WHALE, FIN WHALE
(*Balaenoptera physalus*)

average length: 60.8 feet

This large, slender baleen whale is the most common big whale in the Gulf of Maine, reaching a length of 70 feet and a weight of 50 to 60 tons. The back is dark and the undersides are light, including the lower sides of the flukes and flippers. As its name suggests, this whale has a prominent dorsal fin, which is larger than a blue's, but is often relatively shorter than the taller, sickle-shaped fins of the sei or minke whales. However, identification of the species by fin shape is not reliable, because the fins of individual whales vary somewhat in size and shape, and there is overlap in the fin shapes of these four species.

FINBACK WHALES

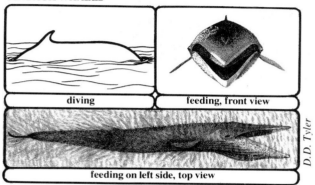

diving

feeding, front view

feeding on left side, top view

D.D. Tyler

The most definite field mark for this species is the uneven coloration of the baleen and lips. On the left side both the lips and baleen are the same dark color as the back. However, on the right side the lower lip, upper lip (sometimes), and the first third of the baleen are white or pale gray. The rest of the baleen is dark with some light streaks. Given the chance, you should always try to maneuver to the right side of a large whale in order to look for this field mark. The white color of the right lips continues as a broad pale wash, which sweeps up from the corner of the jaw to behind the blowhole. Two pale stripes called "chevrons" originate behind the blowhole and run aft, forming a broad "V" along the back and upper sides. When starting a dive, the finback usually shows a considerable length of back posterior to the dorsal fin, as its name suggests.

Finback whales appear to migrate north along the New England coast during the spring and summer, then move south or out to sea during the winter. Their migrations are somewhat irregular and may depend on the local availability of schools of small fish, which are their main food. The two inch long shrimp-like euphausiid crustaceans called "krill" are also eaten if abundant. Finback whales have been observed swimming on their sides circling around or through a school of fish. Some biologists have speculated that the white coloration of the right side of the head is used to startle fish and herd them into a confined area to make feeding easier. However, another scientist suggests that the uneven coloration of the head may serve as camouflage to hide the whale from the fish it pursues. While feeding, the whales often blow 3 or 4 times at equal intervals, dive for 5 to 10 minutes, then reappear at the surface. The spout can be high (10 to 20 feet) and vertical on a windless day.

Information about finback whales in other areas suggest that calving occurs between December and April, after a pregnancy of nearly one year. The 20-foot long calves nurse for seven months and are about 36 feet long at weaning. Young whales feed on planktonic crustaceans, such as copepods ("red feed"), before assuming the adult diet of fish. Finbacks start to mate when about five years old and females may bear a calf every other year. It is estimated that there are about 7200 finback whales in the western North Atlantic, but precise figures are not yet available, nor is there an estimate of the numbers which visit the Gulf of Maine.

John Quinn

MINKE WHALE
(*Balaenoptera acutorostrata*)

average length: 27.8 feet

The minke (pronounced "min-ke") is the smallest of the baleen whales in our area, where it is reported fairly frequently. It is shaped very much like the finback and sei whales, but it is usually only 15 to 30 feet long. The minke whale is dark above, light below, and has yellowish-white baleen plates which are less than 8 inches long. The best field mark for identifying this whale is the broad white band running across each flipper.

MINKE WHALE

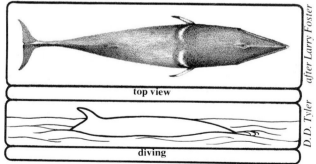

top view

diving

after Larry Foster

D.D. Tyler

Furthermore, a broad light crescent-shaped streak can be seen running from near the blowhole down to the base of each flipper. The following less-definitive field marks may be useful. The sharply pointed snout may sometimes be seen. The fin of the minke may be strongly curved or sickle-shaped, with its pointed tip directed backwards. The spout and fin of this species appear more simultaneously than in the blue, finback, or humpback whales, which may be merely a function of the small size of individuals.

The minke can be an acrobatic whale, and is sometimes seen jumping out of the water (breaching). In addition, these whales seem to have little fear of ships, often coming very close to small craft. Minkes generally travel alone or in pairs and sometimes come quite close to shore. Areas of cold, turbulent waters have been said to be attractive to this species.

The minke whale is widely distributed in the North Atlantic Ocean from the subtropics to Labrador and Newfoundland. The northwest Atlantic population winters offshore and south to Florida, and summers from Cape Cod north. Although this species has often been reported from the Gulf of Maine, nearly all stranded individuals from this area and further south have been immature, whereas strandings from more northerly areas include many mature specimens. Reports indicate that minke whales perform seasonal migrations, but that these are not well understood. Some appear to travel past Nova Scotia in May, reaching Newfoundland in June and northern Labrador in August.

Mating appears to occur in winter or early spring. Females mature when about 24 feet long and 4 years old, then bear a 9-foot calf each year or two, probably during December to February, after 10 to 11 months of pregnancy.

Maximum weight of a minke whale is about 11 tons. No estimates of lifespan are available.

Of all the baleen whales, the minke shows the greatest dependence on fish as food. Herring, capelin, cod, pollack, salmon and other fish are eaten, in addition to some squid and crustaceans. While pursuing fish it will frequent bays, harbors and shallow water, where it sometimes becomes entangled in fishing gear.

A recent estimate suggests that the population of this whale in the western North Atlantic is less than 46,000.

HUMPBACK WHALE
(Megaptera novaeangliae)

The humpback whale, which is relatively common in the Gulf of Maine, has a marvelous set of field marks that make it perhaps the easiest baleen whale to identify in the field.

Averaging about 48 feet in length, the humpback is less slender than the other baleen whales, though most drawings of the animal exaggerate its stoutness. Coloration varies, but humpbacks are generally dark above, and light below. The very long white flippers are unmistakable fieldmarks. The head, snout and flippers bear many knob-like swellings that make it look like the head, as one scientist puts it, is held together with stovebolts. The back is

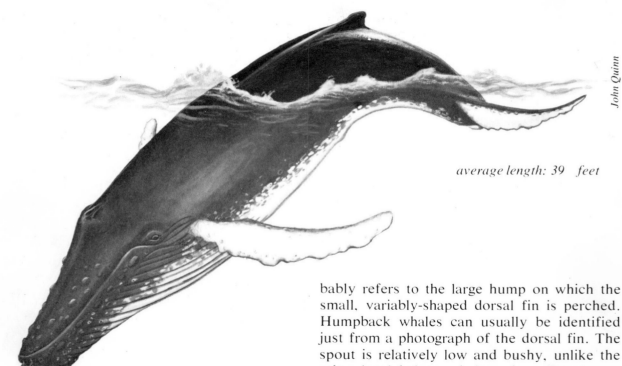

John Quinn

average length: 39 feet

bably refers to the large hump on which the small, variably-shaped dorsal fin is perched. Humpback whales can usually be identified just from a photograph of the dorsal fin. The spout is relatively low and bushy, unlike the other local baleen whales whose spouts are usually high and vertical when seen on a windless day. The flukes, often seen when the whale dives, have irregularly scalloped trailing

generally rounded when the whale is preparing to dive; however, the name ''humpback'' pro-

edges. The amount of white on the underside of the flukes is slightly different in each individual. Similarly, the pattern of black pigmentation near the base of the flipper also may vary among individuals. Individuals can be recognized on the basis of these patterns. Photographs of the underside of the flukes and

HUMPBACK WHALES

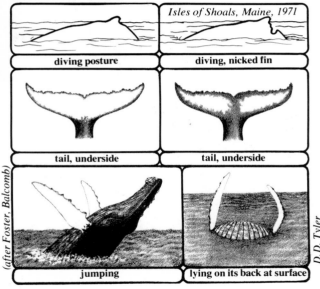

diving posture

Isles of Shoals, Maine, 1971

diving, nicked fin

tail, underside

tail, underside

(after Foster, Balcomb)

jumping

lying on its back at surface

D.D. Tyler

of the flippers are thus especially valuable because they may help to reveal the migrations and behavior of individual whales.

The behavior of this whale is also helpful for identification. It is the most acrobatic of the large whales, and often may be seen breaching (jumping out of the water); rolling on the water surface; holding one or two flippers out of the water; or slapping the water with its flipper or tail. On the southern portions of their western Atlantic range (West Indies to Greenland), these whales produce a variety of sounds, which can be heard on the remarkable record album "Songs of the Humpback Whale" (Capital Records, 1970). However, there is no evidence that they make such complex sounds in the Gulf of Maine or in other northern waters. The meaning of these whale sounds is not yet known.

Humpbacks are seen fairly often in the Gulf of Maine. They have been seen as close as one-half mile from shore traveling alone, in pairs, or in small groups. One group of over a hundred individuals was seen near Portland in the early 19th century, and during early September, 1904, over a hundred were seen on a cruise from the Isles of Shoals to Nova Scotia. Sometimes humpbacks tolerate the presence of boats or even approach a boat. They feed on planktonic crustaceans, especially euphausiids ("krill") and fish (mackerel, capelin or herring), taking in large mouthfuls of food and water, then discharging the water before swallowing the food. Individual humpback whales have been observed to patrol local areas in a regular feeding pattern for a week or more at a time.

The total world population of humpback whales, which are found in nearly all oceans, is estimated to be under 10,000. Before whaling started, the western North Atlantic is estimated to have contained about 1500 humpbacks. Recent estimates of the population suggest that about 1200 humpbacks now inhabit this area, of which about 1000 winter in the Caribbean region. The species includes perhaps a dozen separate populations with little interchange of individuals between them. The number of separate populations in the Atlantic Ocean is not yet known. In general, humpback whales

perform seasonal migrations along partly defined routes which are sometimes close to the coast, moving poleward in spring and summer, then returning to warm-water breeding grounds, such as near Bermuda or in the Caribbean region, where they spend winter and early spring. In the past, large herds have first appeared offshore from Massachusetts to Maine during April and May, and individuals have remained in the Gulf of Maine as late as October or November. The exact migration routes and ranges of individual humpbacks and of the different herds or populations are not yet known.

Data from other areas indicate that females may ovulate up to five times per year, but usually bear one calf every 2 or 3 years. Pregnancy lasts 11 to 12 months, and the 15-foot long calf nurses for up to a year, growing at the rate of up to 1.5 feet per month. The maternal instinct is very strong and mothers will not abandon babies even in extreme danger.The long flippers are sometimes used by a mother to guide the swimming of her calf. Calves are about 25 to 28 feet long at weaning. The age of first breeding is not well known.

John Quinn

average length: 44 feet

RIGHT WHALE
(Eubalaena glacialis)

Rare now, though common in the past, this animal belongs to the family of baleen whales which includes the Bowhead Whale and the Pygmy Right Whale, neither of which occurs in our area.

Adult right whales are between 35 and 50 feet long. The fat body is dark, sometimes black, but often varying shades of brown, and is occasionally mottled with light spots. The flukes are broad with smooth, curved hind edges and pointed tips, and are sometimes held straight up in the air at the beginning of a dive or occasionally while the whale remains under the surface. The rear part of the body just forward of the flukes can then be seen to be thick and round, whereas in the blue whale and its relatives it is thick when seen from the sides, but very thin when viewed straight on.

Unlike any of the other baleen whales found in the Gulf of Maine, the right whale has no dorsal fin. When observed from fore or aft, the spout can be seen to be divided into two distinct portions, because the two nostrils are widely separated in this whale. Light-colored, wart-like growths called ''callosities'' are located on the front of the strongly-arched upper jaw and at other places around the blowhole, eye, and along the lower jaw. The

RIGHT WHALE

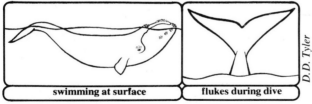

swimming at surface | flukes during dive

D.D. Tyler

variable pattern of these light-colored patches has been used to identify individuals in the closely-related southern hemisphere right whale, and might prove useful in our area. There are no grooves on the throat and chest.

The right whale usually is relatively slow and sluggish. It strains small planktonic copepods

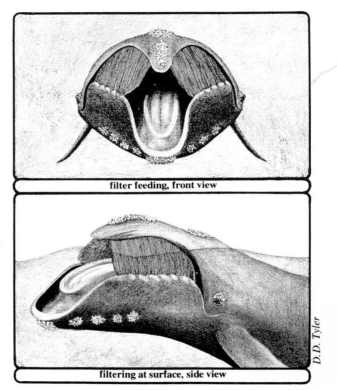

filter feeding, front view

filtering at surface, side view

D.D. Tyler

and other crustaceans from the water through its fine baleen, which is dark in color and up to

7 feet long. In contrast to the finback whale and its relatives, which strain larger food items from single large gulps of water, a feeding right whale strains small food organisms continuously while swimming, sometimes near the surface. Water enters the mouth through the opening between the series of baleen plates on the left and right sides, then passes out through the baleen, leaving the food particles on the inside surface of the plates. Right whale spouts may be hard to see owing to the slow regular breathing rate (one breath every minute or two), but the breathing pattern may be helpful in identifying this species.

The right whale's range includes the temperate waters of the North Atlantic Ocean from Florida to the Gulf of St. Lawrence. As a result of overhunting in the 17th and 18th centuries, it is now rare throughout the range and the population is estimated to be a few hundred. Historical records indicate that in the New England area it used to be most common during late autumn, winter and spring. Right whales probably migrate north along the New England coast starting in January and continuing through to April or nearly May, but the destination of their migration is not known. Probably many right whales bypass the inshore waters of the Gulf of Maine. During summer and autumn, members of the population return to warmer waters, probably including Florida, Bermuda, the coasts of Georgia and the Carolinas, and possibly Massachusetts Bay. However, the migration routes of individuals or particular herds are not known. A group of up to 20 or 30 can be seen in Cape Cod Bay during spring, and individuals can occasionally be sighted from shore vantage points. Right whales have also been seen recently during summer near Eastport and Mt. Desert Rock, Maine. Perhaps as a result of their small population size, right whales are usually seen alone or in small groups. This species has been protected from hunting by international agreements since 1937, and the herd may be increasing slowly. Perhaps larger groups will begin to be seen in the future.

Mating takes place from April to July, and newborn calves, about 13 to 18 feet long, are born from January to March, after a pregnancy of about one year. Pregnant females tend to remain apart from the other animals, and calving probably occurs in quiet waters near shore. The exact location of calving grounds is not known. Females have strong maternal instincts and will not abandon sucklings. Juveniles may become sexually mature at 3 to 5 years of age. The average lifespan is not known.

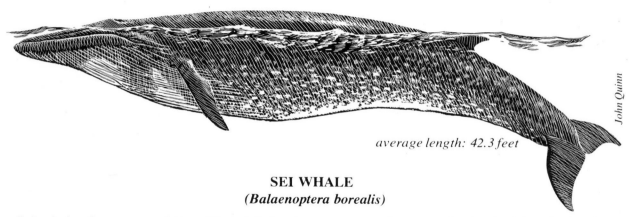

average length: 42.3 feet

John Quinn

SEI WHALE
(*Balaenoptera borealis*)

Sei whales (pronounced ''say'') and finback whales are easily confused. The sei is smaller, 50 feet at the longest. Like the finback whale, it has a prominent dorsal fin, is dark above and light below, and has a high vertical spout. The flanks of the sei whale usually have light spots, however (unlike the blue whale) the spots do not extend across the back. The flank of the finback whale, in contrast, is uniformly dark, except for the light stripe from the flipper to the blowhole. The flukes are dark underneath, but are usually not shown when the whale dives. Although the shape of the dorsal fin can be identical in some sei and finback whales, it is usually relatively taller, thinner and more sickle-shaped in the sei. The fin may break water very shortly after the spout is seen.

Sighting reports of the sei whale are rare from the Gulf of Maine, perhaps partly because observers do not usually discriminate between sei and finback whales. No population data are available. A large group of sei whales is reported to frequent the area southeast of Cape Sable, Nova Scotia. It is possible that the species normally bypasses the Gulf of Maine during migrations. This species tends to feed on small planktonic crustaceans, especially copepods, and the baleen, which is black with a fringe of white bristles, is very fine allowing the whale to filter these small animals. Sei whales have sometimes been seen to swim slowly, just below the surface, with mouths slightly opened, skimming plankton and covering several hundred feet between breaths. When feeding near the surface, the breathing rate of sei whales is often slow and regular. A single breath will be followed by perhaps 3 or 4 minutes of feeding and then

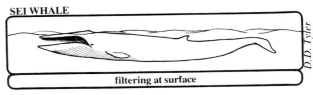

SEI WHALE

filtering at surface

D.D. Tyler

another breath. When spouting in this pattern, a sei whale might be harder to notice than a whale which spouts several times in succession. However, a sei whale may also dive for food or pursue fish, at which time its breathing pattern might be similar to that of other baleen whales. Data from other areas suggest that sei whales mate in January and February. Pregnancy lasts ten to twelve months, and the 15-foot calf nurses for about seven months, growing at the rate of nearly one inch in length per day. These whales may begin to mate when between 40 and 45 feet long, and females may bear a calf every second year. A sei whale may live to be 70 years old.

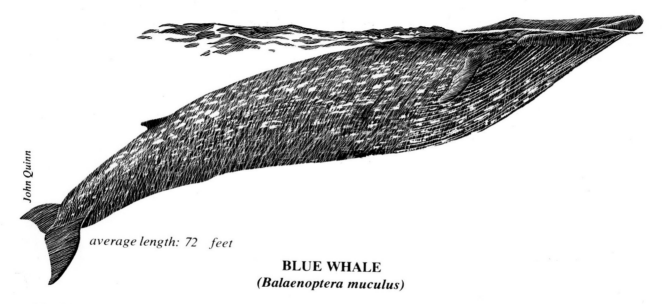

John Quinn

average length: 72   feet

BLUE WHALE
(Balaenoptera muculus)

The blue whale is the largest animal living to-day, and is thought to be the largest that has ever lived. The length averages 73 feet, but the record was a female 99 feet long and supposed to have weighed 150 tons. The whale is a pale blue-grey, mottled with light spots on the sides, back and belly. Although the sei whale also has light spots, they are usually confined to the sides and are not found on the animal's back. The dorsal fin is relatively small and is situated far back on the body. The undersides of the flippers and flukes are light-colored. Although the flukes sometimes may be seen when the whale is sounding (diving), they are seldom raised at an angle of more than 45 degrees to the water. The top portion of the head and snout is broader in the blue whale than in the finback and sei whales. In addition

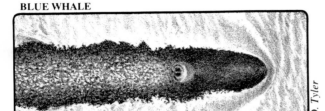

D.D. Tyler

broad head, top view

to the reliable field marks mentioned above, the tall straight spout and the long interval (2-3 seconds) between the spout and the appearance of the dorsal fin may sometimes aid in identification of this species.

The blue whale strains krill from the water using its black baleen. A medium-sized blue whale weighing 70 tons probably eats several tons of these plankton animals per day. Baby blue whales are about 23 feet long and weigh up to 5,000 pounds. They gain nearly 200 pounds per day during nursing, which lasts about one year. Females give birth every two or three years, following a pregnancy of about one year. The age at onset of sexual maturity is not well known, but has been estimated at between 5 and 10 years. Blue whales supposedly can live to be nearly 100 years old. During the past few years, fears have often been expressed that this species might become extinct as a result of excessive hunting. The latest estimates suggest that perhaps 15,000 blue whales still exist throughout the range, which includes the Atlantic, Pacific, Indian and Antarctic Oceans. Within the western North Atlantic Ocean, a population of perhaps a few hundred blues may still be seen around Newfoundland, on the Grand Bank, in the Gulf of St. Lawrence, and possibly along the outer banks fringing the Gulf of Maine. The pre-whaling population in this area has been estimated to be about 1100 whales. Blue whales have been protected from hunting in all regions since 1967 by the International Whaling Commission, and the stocks appear to be increasing slowly. Although it may take more than 50 years for the populations to approach pre-whaling abundance, blue whales appear to have escaped extinction.

Within the Gulf of Maine, blue whales would be sighted only rarely. No definite sighting report has been published; however, one publication says that blues are occasionally sighted at the mouth of Passamaquoddy Bay. Probably one reason for its rarity in our area is that it prefers waters which are higher in the production of krill.

SPECIES ACCOUNTS, TOOTHED WHALES

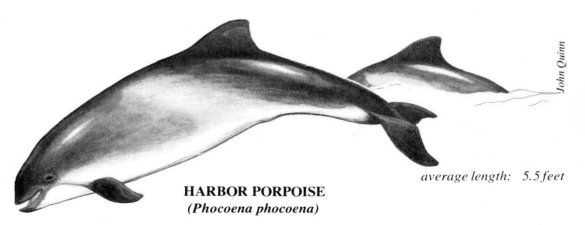

John Quinn

average length: 5.5 feet

HARBOR PORPOISE
(*Phocoena phocoena*)

This little porpoise is the most frequently seen cetacean in the Gulf of Maine. It is one of the smallest of the cetaceans, reaching a length of only 6 feet and a weight of perhaps 120 pounds. The back, head, flippers and flukes may appear dark gray, greenish brown or nearly black. The undersides are lighter, from white to dark gray, and a light gray patch is visible in front of the dorsal fin. The fin is triangular (rather than curved or sickle-shaped) and the sloped trailing edge is only slightly curved. No beak is visible externally. The teeth are flattened and spade-shaped.

The harbor porpoise can swim very quickly, but does not usually jump. Sometimes it will lie quietly at the surface. Usually it ignores or avoids boats. It generally breathes 3 to 4 times at intervals of 2 to 30 seconds, then dives for 3 to 4 minutes, but it does not make a visible spout. It is often seen in groups of varying sizes, usually in July, August and September, and usually close to land or in shallow water, where it feeds on bottom-living fishes or invertebrates and on schooling fish such as her-

ring or mackerel. This species often swims up rivers. Harbor porpoises probably migrate off-shore in winter.

HARBOR PORPOISE

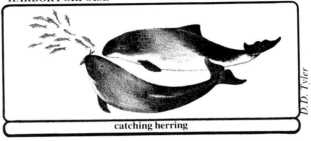

catching herring

Young are born from April through July after eleven months of pregnancy. Nursing lasts up to eight months. Sexual maturity is reached in 3 to 4 years and these porpoises may live to be up to 20 years old.

POTHEAD, BLACKFISH, PILOT WHALE
(Globicephala melaena)

This medium-sized whale (up to 20 feet long and 3 tons in weight) is moderately common in the Gulf of Maine, and is seen in groups of five to several hundred. It is entirely black except

for a light-colored, anchor-shaped patch (only rarely visible at sea) at the base of the flippers, on the throat and chest, and occasionally farther aft. The dorsal fin is high, strongly

average length: 13.7 feet

John Quinn

curved, rounded, set fairly far forward on the back and — most important — noticeably longer at the base than at the top. The high, rounded melon overhangs the snout in older animals, making the whale look like it has a pot or kettle upside down on its head. Potheads are similar to gray grampuses in size; however, the bulbous melon, unmarked jet black color and long-based fin are clear field marks for the pothead.

Potheads are frequently found stranded on beaches, occasionally in large numbers (a herd of 1975 animals stranded at Wellfleet, Massachusetts in 1895 and about 3000 beached on Cape Cod in 1874). Although the cause is not known, some sources suspect that the whale is unable to detect a very gradual slope of the bottom. Other scientists are investigating the possibility that the whale's orientation ability could be harmed by parasites in the inner ear. In any case, these whales have a strong tendency to follow a leader, and if the leader becomes stranded, the rest often seem to follow.

Potheads feed mainly on squid, but also take some fish and small invertebrates. They appear

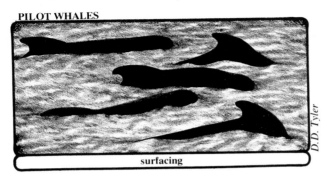

PILOT WHALES

D.D. Tyler

surfacing

to spend winters in warmer waters of the North Atlantic, offshore from the continental shelf.

During summer, they follow schools of squid into northern waters and their exact distribution appears to be determined by the movements of the squid. Written reports suggest that potheads are more common around Newfoundland than in our area. This species sometimes enters bays or approaches the coast during summer.

Females mature sexually at about age 6 and males at about age 13. Between ages 6 and 18, a female will produce about 5 or 6 single calves, each about 5.5 feet long at birth. Pregnancy and nursing each last one year, and the young are born during summer. The maximum lifespan has been estimated at 25 years.

WHITE-SIDED DOLPHIN
(Lagenorhynchus acutus)

The white-sided dolphin ranges in size from 6.5 to 9 feet. At sea, it would appear to be about the same size and shape as the white-beaked dolphin. The dorsal fin, back, flippers and flukes are all black. Between the black of the back and the white of the belly, the sides are gray except for the key field mark, which is a narrow white patch beginning below the dorsal fin and running aft. At close range, a streak of yellow or tan can be seen lying im-

John Quinn

average length: 7.7 feet

mediately above the white patch and running up toward (but not over) the ridge of the tail. Observers should have little difficulty in differentiating this species from the white-beaked dolphin if sufficient attention is paid to the markings on the sides of the animals.

On September 8, 1974, up to 500 or 1000 individuals of this species were reported to be chasing herring in Longley Cove, near Den-nysville, Maine. About 100 animals, including many pregnant or nursing mothers, were stranded on the ebb tide and died. Many of their bodies are being studied by the New England Aquarium. This is the largest sighting (and stranding) from the Gulf of Maine for this species. The white-sided dolphin is not frequently reported in the Gulf of Maine, perhaps because people are not very good at identifying it. Probably it stays offshore much of the time; however, it is reported to be common just off Cape Cod beaches from Plymouth to Provincetown in the spring.

John Quinn

WHITE-BEAKED DOLPHIN
(Lagenorhynchus albirostris)

average length: 9.3 feet

This dolphin grows to about 9 feet in length. Despite its name, the beak is often dark in western North Atlantic populations. Although this species appears to be about the same size as the white-sided dolphin, it is more strikingly patterned. White patches are found above the flippers, around the blowhole, and along the sides. The patches on the sides begin forward of the dorsal fin, sweep down and back, then spread up along the entire rear of the body and over the back and tail. The dorsal fin, flippers and flukes are black, and the belly is white. There is always a sharp edge between the black and white portions of the body. At sea, the white hind end of this species is an excellent field mark.

The white-beaked dolphin may prefer more northerly, colder waters than those in the Gulf of Maine; however, individuals are sometimes seen offshore in our area and they are common off Cape Cod in the spring. They are active animals and it is possible to get a good look at them, for they frequently jump completely out of the water. White-beaked dolphins feed on squid, fish and small crustaceans. Relatively little is known of other aspects of their biology.

SADDLEBACK DOLPHIN, COMMON DOLPHIN
(*Delphinus delphis*)

This small dolphin reaches a length of 8.5 feet. It is black above and white on the belly, with a distinctive "crisscross" or figure-eight pattern of light gray or ochre running along the sides. Fishermen in Newfoundland call this species the saddleback dolphin, owing to the black saddle above the gray crisscross. At the rear of the slender, elongated beak, a whitish band runs across the front of the melon. A narrow black mask in the center of the white band connects the black eye-rings. A black band runs from the chin to the front edge of the flipper.

average length: 6.8 feet

Although this species is one of the most numerous dolphins in the world, it is not frequently reported in the Gulf of Maine, perhaps for two reasons. First, it is usually found offshore in deep water (although individuals are occasionally reported near land). Second, it is more common in warm-water regions, where large schools are often seen. Travelers on the *MV Bluenose, MV Bolero, MV Prince of Fundy* or other offshore vessels may see occasional groups of saddlebacks. In contrast to the harbor porpoise, they often leap high out of the water and play in front of ships.

Saddleback dolphins feed mainly on schooling fish of a variety of species, although they

SADDLEBACK DOLPHINS

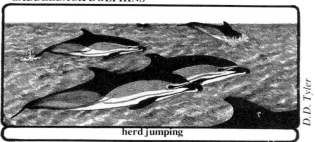

herd jumping

D.D. Tyler

sometimes eat squid. A full-grown individual might eat between 10 and 20 pounds of food per day. Information from other locations suggests that females give birth to one calf each year after 11 months of pregnancy. Nursing lasts for 4 months and calves may begin to mate at age three years. Individuals may live 25 to 30 years.

KILLER WHALE
(Orcinus orca)

This is a very striking and beautiful medium-sized whale which may reach nearly 30 feet in length. The killer whale is black above and white below, with a sharp division between the two areas. An oval white patch is located above and behind each eye, and there is a gray saddle behind the dorsal fin, especially in adult animals. The white of the belly extends part way up along the rear flank. The tall dorsal fin is one of the killer whale's most distinctive features, sometimes being as high as five feet in old males, but lower in females. Fins of younger animals of both sexes are alike. The black flippers are broad and paddle-like, and can sometimes be seen as the whale swims.

KILLER WHALES

swimming males (tall, straight fins) and females (curved fins)

D.D. Tyler

John Quinn

average length: male—23 feet, female—19 feet

Killer whales are found in all oceans. They are most common in cooler waters and in productive coastal waters. They are not reported frequently from the Gulf of Maine, although they have been seen in small groups on some occasions. In other areas the distribution and migrations of killer whales appear to be related to the movements of baleen whales and of herring. Killer whales feed on fish (cod, flatfish, herring), squid, octopus, sea birds, and marine mammals (including porpoises, young whales and seals). They have often been seen to hunt in groups, apparently using strategy and coordinated movements to overcome large whales or to herd prey.

The reproductive biology of this species is not known for our area. In the North Pacific, mating may take place all year around with a peak during May to July, and births may be concentrated in late summer or autumn, after a pregnancy of 13 to 16 months. No data are available for western Atlantic populations. Newborn calves are up to 9 feet long and weigh about 400 pounds. They nurse for about a year, during which time females and young appear to stay slightly separated from bachelors and bulls. By age four, females are sexually mature, but no estimates are available for males. Adult males weigh about 9 tons, and females 4.5 tons. Killer whales are known to live longer than 35 years, and deterioration of the teeth with age may be a contributing cause of death.

Despite their name and reputation, killer whales do not seem to present a serious threat to human welfare. There are no documented reports of killer whales maliciously attacking humans at sea. Killer whales have been maintained and trained successfully in aquariums, where they seem to be gentle and affectionate to their trainers. A phonograph recording utilizing some of the sounds produced by killer whales in captivity is available (Paul Horne, "Inside Two," Epic No. 31600). Despite the fact that these whales are not particularly dangerous to humans, they should be treated with caution and respect, as should all marine mammals.

BOTTLENOSE DOLPHIN
(*Tursiops truncatus*)

Of all the smaller cetaceans, the bottlenose dolphin is most familiar to the public. As a result of its availability in inshore waters, trainability, and the relative ease with which it adjusts to captivity, this dolphin has been captured and placed in aquariums all across the country. Other bottlenose dolphins, such as "Flipper" have appeared in television shows or movies, while some, most notably "Tuffy," have been trained to help scuba divers.

average length: 10.5 feet

The length of this dolphin is usually 8 to 12 feet. It is bluish gray above and slightly lighter below, but there is no distinct color pattern. The melon is rounded, but does not bulge and the jaws are drawn out into a short beak. The large, curved dorsal fin is located on the middle of the back.

Bottlenose dolphins are seen rarely in New England waters. They are more common in warmer, more southerly waters, where they often travel in groups of up to 100 individuals, and are most common in coastal waters, where they frequently may be seen jumping and sporting about. In the Gulf of Maine, they would probably appear in smaller groups.

This species hunts bottom fishes and squids by echo-location. It breeds during the warmer months. Pregnancy lasts about eleven months and nursing six months. Strong social bonds are formed between pairs and between mothers and calves. Bottlenose dolphins may live to be twenty-five years old.

average length: 12.3 feet

John Quinn

GRAY GRAMPUS

(Grampus griseus)

Growing to a length of 13.5 feet, this gray and white dolphin has a high, narrow, curved, sharply-pointed dorsal fin that is somewhat similar to the fin of a killer whale. It always has numerous white scratches (cause unknown) all over its body. The front of the head is blunt.

This species has been seen to jump clear of the water. It is most common in warm, offshore waters and is rare in the Gulf of Maine. Squid is its main food, but little else is known of its biology.

STRIPED DOLPHIN
(Stenella coeruleoalba)

The striped dolphin grows to a maximum length of about 9 feet, but averages about 6 or 7 feet. The best field mark for this species is the "bilge stripe," a black line which runs along the white lower side from eye to anus. Above the bilge stripe, a light gray or white patch sweeps back from the eye, sends a branch up toward the dorsal fin, and continues back along the side and up toward the ridge of the back. The tall, curved, triangular dorsal fin is pointed and is located nearly at midbody, as in most dolphins.

This species is known to inhabit the warmer waters of both the Atlantic and Pacific Oceans, although it has been reported as far north as Greenland. It is probably a rare visitor to the Gulf of Maine. Only two specimens have ever been reported here, a young female stranded in Beverly, Massachusetts on January 31, 1975, and a juvenile male found freshly dead on the beach at Falmouth, Maine, February 13, 1975. None have been recorded on the eastern Canadian coast, however, specimens have been seen both at sea and stranded at Sable Island, suggesting that in the western North Atlantic the species is normally restricted to Gulf Stream or continental slope waters. This dolphin, which used to be known as *Stenella styx*, has also been recorded along the southeastern U.S. coast, along the Gulf Coast of Florida, and near Jamaica.

John Quinn

average length: 7.2 feet

The biology of this species in the western North Atlantic is poorly known. In the waters around Japan, where it occurs in large schools and is hunted for food, it reaches sexual maturity at about four years of age and slightly under 6 feet in length. Mating takes place both in spring and autumn, and calves are born the following year. Squid is its main food in those waters.

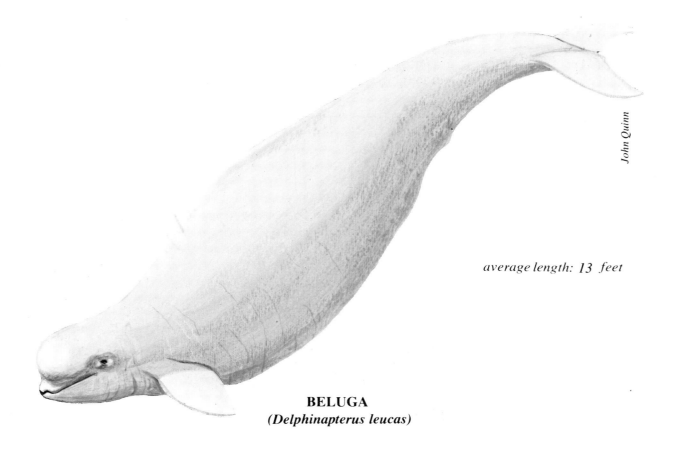

average length: 13 feet

BELUGA
(Delphinapterus leucas)

The adult beluga is about 11 feet (female) to 13 feet (male) long and is entirely white. The calves are born brown, then turn gray, and finally lighten to white in about their tenth year of life. Probably the white color of the adult is an adaptation to life in arctic seas, where this species normally lives, allowing it to hide among ice floes from predators and perhaps to reduce the amount of heat loss from its body. The beluga has a rounded melon, no beak, and no dorsal fin. The jaws contain sharp, pointed teeth. This species has been called the "sea canary" because its high-pitched squeaks, trills and whistles can sometimes be heard through the hull of a boat.

In their northern habitats, belugas travel in groups of up to several hundred animals. The individuals or groups of two or three belugas which have been seen on occasion along the New England coast as far south as the Cape Cod canal (and even Long Island Sound) probably have strayed from the population of about 1,000 which lives in the St. Lawrence River.

Belugas are polygamous and breed in the spring. Females bear a calf every second or third year after a 13 to 14 month pregnancy. Calves weigh about 170 pounds and are about 5 feet long. Following a year of nursing, they begin to hunt for food, but continue to suckle until weaning at age two. Females with calves stay in herds separate from males. Females mature sexually at age 5 and males at age 8. Belugas have a diverse diet which includes many species of fish, squid, crabs, shrimp, clams and worms. They tend to feed on the bottom and can dive to 125 feet to find food. They will also enter fresh water. Belugas have been kept in captivity at some aquariums.

SPERM WHALE
(Physeter catodon)

Sperm whales, immortalized in *Moby Dick*, and the mainstay of the great American whaling fleet during the 18th and 19th centuries, are the largest of the odontocetes. Males may

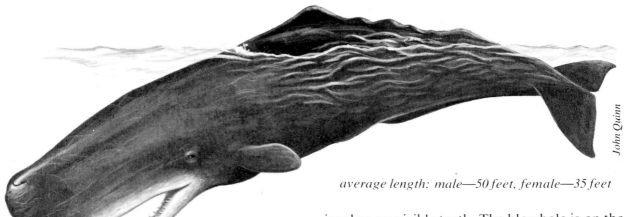

John Quinn

average length: male—50 feet, female—35 feet

reach a length of 60 feet, although 50 feet is more common. Females are a good deal smaller (as is the case in most of the toothed whales), averaging 37 feet.

These whales have a blunt, square head with a long, narrow lower jaw containing up to 30 pairs of large teeth, which used to be the main source of ivory for scrimshaw work. The upper jaw has no visible teeth. The blowhole is on the left side of the front of the head, and the spout is therefore tipped forward and to the left at about a 45 degree angle from the head. Sperm whales occasionally have a very small fin, but usually it is reduced to only a hump set near the back of the body and followed by a series of bumps along the ridge of the tail. They are usually brown (or sometimes slate gray) above, and are paler below. The skin on the sides is often wrinkled or corrugated. The flukes are large and triangular, with smooth edges, rounded tips, and a deep notch in the middle.

Sperm whales are seen only rarely in the Gulf of Maine, although a 35-foot female stranded alive on Mt. Desert Island in October, 1968. In general they appear to prefer deep water and generally stay far out to sea along

SPERM WHALE

D.D. Tyler

seen from rear, single spout tipped forward and left

the edge of the continental shelf, where the species ranges throughout all oceans and from the Equator to high latitudes. Females and young sperm whales generally remain within the area from 45 degrees south to 45 degrees north latitude; however, old males may seasonally venture to higher latitudes. The social structure of sperm whale populations is complex. Females (including pregnant and nursing females), calves and some juveniles gather in groups called "nursery schools," averaging 25 animals in size. After weaning young whales may form "juvenile schools." When males mature sexually at about age 9 they may join "bachelor schools," of up to 10 whales. However, a male does not begin to breed until "socially mature," perhaps at age 25, because all breeding females are controlled by older males. During the breeding season (spring and early summer) males round up females of breeding age (about 8 years and up) into harems of from 10 to several hundred. Battles over females probably occur, and a young male probably will be unable to breed until he defeats a reigning harem bull in battle.

Perhaps every two or three years, after a pregnancy of 12 to 16 months, a female gives birth to a 12-foot long calf, which nurses for up to a year. Mothers defend calves from danger very fiercely.

Squid, especially the larger species, are the main food of sperm whales. They feed mainly at night, but even in the day there is no light at the depths where they often hunt for food. Consequently, sperm whales have been suspected to find food by using sonar. However, it has also been suggested that a sperm whale actually lures squid to its mouth by hanging motionless in the water with its mouth open and attracting them toward the light-colored inner lining of its jaws. The luminescent secretions of a chewed squid might be smeared on the teeth to aid in the process. Photographs of the ocean bottom suggest that sperm whales may at times plow furrows in the bottom at depths down to 3,500 feet, perhaps while feeding. When feeding, sperm whales usually surface in nearly the same location as where they went down, a fact that was used to advantage by old whaling captains. Owing to their general scarcity in our region, they would probably only be seen individually or in twos, except possibly on the outer banks where the species might possibly be seen more frequently at some times of the year.

PYGMY SPERM WHALE
(Kogia breviceps)

This whale has probably never been seen alive in the Gulf of Maine. The sole record in this area is of a dead individual at Nahant, Mass., in 1910; however, another specimen was found dead at Sable Island, in 1969, and a third under ice in Halifax Harbor during the winter of 1970. This whale looks superficially like a miniature (up to 13 feet long) sperm whale because of its narrow lower jaw and toothless upper jaw. However, the front of the head is more pointed (shark-like) than that of its larger relative, the blowhole is on top of its head, and it has a small, but distinct dorsal fin like a dolphin. Coloration is dark gray above and light gray below. The flippers are relatively large (1/6 body length) and rounded. The

(PYGMY SPERM WHALE)

John Quinn

average length 10 feet

pygmy sperm whale is found both in warm and cool waters, but its occurrence in the Gulf of Maine is probably accidental. Pygmy sperm whales are reported to eat squid, crabs and shrimp, but little is known of their biology.

NORTHERN BOTTLENOSE WHALE
(Hyperoodon ampullatus)

Adults of this medium-sized whale grow to about 29 feet (males) or 26 feet (females) in length. Observers who have been fortunate enough to see them at sea usually describe the

John Quinn

average length: male—26 feet, female—24 feet

color as brown. Smaller animals appear to be a uniform chocolate brown, while larger ones develop varying amounts of light or yellow color. A large, old specimen (especially a male) may develop a cream-colored head and a high, bulging melon. When seen at sea, these whales appear to have a slight, faintly gray depression or ''neck'' behind the melon. As is the case in all members of the family Ziphiidae (commonly called the beaked whales) the elongation of the jaws is visible externally as a short beak. None of the beaked whales have more than two pairs of teeth. This species has one or two pairs of teeth located at the tip of the lower jaw and none in the upper jaw. The teeth may not be functional and they sometimes fail to erupt through the gums. The curved dorsal fin is somewhat shorter than in a baleen whale, although it is of comparable shape.

This species is limited to the northern North Atlantic Ocean, but it is usually seen only in deep water such as along the edge of the continental shelf off the coast of Nova Scotia and around Sable Island, mainly in early summer. Within the Gulf of Maine, dead bottlenose whales have been found stranded at North Dennis, Mass. (1869); Wells Beach, Maine (1906) and Cobequid Bay, Nova Scotia (1969); but no live sightings have been reported.

These whales appear to travel in small groups of up to ten individuals. They have sometimes been reported to be playful. Observers have reported that they will sometimes approach a ship stopped in deep water if some noise is made, such as banging on the hull or leaving a generator running. The main food of bottlenose whales is squid and some fish.

The bottlenose whale and the two beaked whales known from our area will probably never be seen by most whalewatchers. They are included in this guide more for the sake of completeness than in the hope that these brief descriptions could enable a novice to identify a specimen at sea. Nevertheless, perhaps these descriptions might lead to a report of a stranding which would otherwise have gone unrecorded.

TRUE'S BEAKED WHALE

This species has been reported only once in the Gulf of Maine, as a dead specimen stranded at Wells Beach, Maine, in 1937. It seems to be rare throughout the North Atlantic Ocean, which appears to be its main range. The length averages 17 feet. The short beak contains only two, small flattened teeth, which are located at the tip of the lower jaw. The upper jaw is toothless.

Although this whale has probably not been seen alive often enough to permit an accurate description of its coloration, it is said to be black above and gray below with dark flippers. The dorsal fin is very small and is placed three-quarters of the way back on the body. Essentially nothing is known of its biology. The stomachs of beached specimens have contained squid and sometimes fish.

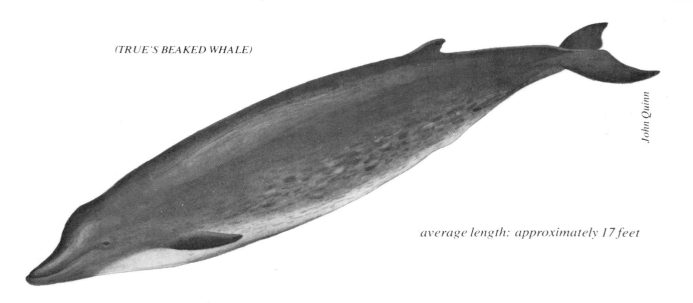

(TRUE'S BEAKED WHALE)

average length: approximately 17 feet

John Quinn

DENSE-BEAKED WHALE
(Mesoplodon densirostris)

Although this species has been found in all oceans having tropical or warm temperate waters, it is apparently very rare throughout all of its known range, and its biology is very

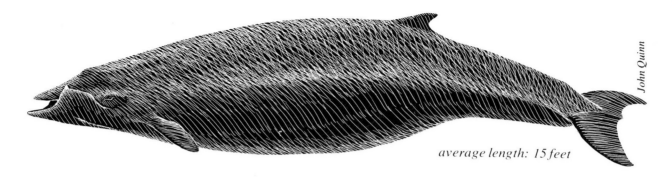

John Quinn

average length: 15 feet

poorly understood. No live sightings have ever been reported from the Gulf of Maine. However, a stranded specimen was identified dead on the beach at Annisquam, Massachusetts in 1898 and another corpse was found slightly outside of our study area at Peggy's Cove, Nova Scotia, in 1940. The average length of this species appears to be 14 to 16 feet. The small, triangular dorsal fin is located just behind mid-body, with its sharp point directed backwards. The flippers are small and the flukes do not have a central notch. There are only two teeth, each of which is very wide and flat, about 6 inches long, and positioned on a large, wedge-shaped prominence on the side of the lower jaw. Observations on a stranded specimen in New Jersey indicated that the breath may be directed forward over the beak instead of straight up into the air. If so, this species would be hard to notice at sea.

KEY FOR THE IDENTIFICATION

OF STRANDED WHALES, DOLPHINS AND PORPOISES IN THE GULF OF MAINE

I. Baleen in upper jaw (may be rotted out in dead specimens). No teeth. Usually over 30 feet long (except minke whale and juveniles). Continue to A. BALEEN WHALES.

II. Baleen absent, teeth present though not always visible above gums. Usually well under 30 feet long (except sperm whale and largest male killer and northern bottlenosed whales). Continue to B. TOOTHED WHALES.

A. BALEEN WHALES (MYSTICETES)

1.   **a.** Dorsal fin and throat grooves present. Continue to 2.
    b. Dorsal fin and throat grooves absent. RIGHT WHALE.

2.   **a.** Over thirty feet. Continue to 3.
    b. Under thirty feet, yellowish or cream-colored baleen, white patch on flipper, pointed snout. MINKE WHALE.
    c. Under thirty feet, but not as in 2b. Juvenile baleen whale. Continue to 3.

3.   **a.** Extremely long white flippers, sawtoothed hind edges on flukes, knob-like bumps on head and jaws,

4.   **a.** Length up to 95 feet, relatively small dorsal fin set far back on body; light gray-blue with conspicuous lighter spots on belly, sides and back; black baleen; up to 90 throat grooves reaching to mid-belly. BLUE WHALE.
    b. Length up to 75 feet; prominent dorsal fin; baleen on right side one-third white and two-thirds dark; lower right lip and sometimes upper right lip white; up to 80 throat grooves reaching to mid-belly. FINBACK WHALE.

black baleen, up to 25 throat grooves, to 55 feet. HUMPBACK WHALE.

b. Shorter flippers, smooth edges on flukes, over 25 throat grooves. Continue to 4.

c. Length up to 60 feet; prominent dorsal fin; baleen black with white fringes; light spots often on flanks; up to 60 throat grooves reach only slightly past flipper. SEI WHALE.

B. TOOTHED WHALES (ODONTOCETES)

5. a. Length up to 60 feet (females to 35 feet), massive square head with blowhole at left tip; narrow lower jaw with large teeth; dorsal hump; triangular flukes; sometimes "wrinkled" skin on flanks. SPERM WHALE.

b. Size under 30 feet. Continue to 6.

6. a. Dorsal fin present. Continue to 7.

b. Dorsal fin absent, body all white (juveniles gray or brown). BELUGA.

7. a. Jaws not drawn out into beak. Continue to 8.

b. Jaws extended forward as distinct beak. Continue to 11.

8. a. Small dorsal fin. Continue to 9.

b. Large dorsal fin. Continue to 10.

9. a. Very small (up to 6 feet); small triangular dorsal fin; small, flattened, spade-shaped teeth. HARBOR PORPOISE.

b. Low dorsal fin; dark gray above and light below; large rounded flippers; length to 13 feet; jaw like sperm whale. PYGMY SPERM WHALE.

10. a. Very high dorsal fin; body black above with white patch behind eye, gray saddle behind dorsal fin, and white of belly extending up on sides; rounded paddle-shaped flippers. KILLER WHALE.

b. Rounded bulging forehead overhangs short snout; very long-based, curved, round-tipped dorsal fin set well forward of midbody; curved and pointed flippers; color jet black except for anchor-shaped grey patch on chest; 8-10 teeth on each side of upper and lower jaws, 1/2 inch diameter; length to 20 feet. POTHEAD.

c. Blunt snout; large, curved, pointed dorsal fin; gray body, with many long white scratches or scabs; usually 3-7 teeth on each side of lower jaw, 0-2 in upper, 1/2 inch diameter; length to 14 feet. GRAY GRAMPUS.

11. a. Definite black and white color pattern and/or many teeth in both jaws. Continue to 12.

b. Basically uniform color, usually dark gray, black or brownish; only 2 teeth in lower jaw, none in upper. Continue to 13.

12. a. Body dark above, light below, white patch on side runs aft from below dorsal fin and sweeps over the ridge of the back; short snout, usually black, sometimes white; 22-25 teeth on each side of upper and lower jaws, 1/4 inch diameter; length to 10 feet. WHITE-BEAKED DOLPHIN.

inch diameter; length to 8 feet. SADDLEBACK DOLPHIN.

d. Dark color of upper body separated from white of belly by a distinct dark line running along side from eye to anus; white patch runs from head back and up toward dorsal fin; 43-50 teeth on each side of upper and lower jaws, 1/8 inch diameter; length to 8 feet. STRIPED DOLPHIN.

e. Body gray above, lighter on belly; dark stripes run from base of short beak to eye and blowhole; no distinct color pattern; 22-25 teeth on each side of upper and lower jaws, 1/8 inch diameter; length to 12 feet. BOTTLENOSE DOLPHIN.

13. a. Color gray to light brown or yellowish; large forehead bulges over short beak; two small teeth at tip of lower jaw; light gray indentation between head and rest of body; relatively small curved dorsal fin located behind midpoint of body; length to 30 feet. NORTHERN BOTTLENOSE WHALE.

b. Body dark above, white on belly, white patch on side runs aft from below dorsal fin but does not reach over ridge of back; yellow or tan streak behind white patch; short snout; 30-40 teeth on each side of upper and lower jaws, 3/16 inch diamter; length to 9 feet. WHITE-SIDED DOLPHIN.

c. Dark above, white below, with grey or yellowish criss-cross or figure-eight pattern on sides; dorsal fin curved, triangular and pointed; 40-50 teeth on each side of upper and lower jaws, 1/10

b. Black above, gray on belly; small dorsal fin located toward rear of the body; two small flattened teeth on tip of lower jaw; length to 17 feet. TRUE'S BEAKED WHALE.

c. Body all dark; two large teeth about 6 inches long placed on wedge-shaped prominence near front of lower jaw, with only their tips exposed; high triangular dorsal fin located just behind mid-body; flukes lack central notch; length to 15 feet. DENSE-BEAKED WHALE.

SAMPLE WHALE SIGHTING REPORT FORM

Your Name _____

Address _____

Phone _____

WHALE SIGHTING

REPORT (Form 7 5-1)

Mail To: Allied Whale
College of the Atlantic
Bar Harbor, Maine 04609
Tel. 207-288-5015

I. CONDITIONS

Date _____ _____ , 19 _____   Time _____ am pm

Weather and Sea conditions _____

Observed from boat _____ island _____ shore _____ airplane _____ with binoculars _____

Location _____ (coordinates _____ _____)

2. OBSERVATIONS

How many whales sighted? _____ In a tight school? _____ How far away? _____ Estimated size _____

Heading of animals (magnetic) _____ Estimated speed (knots)_____

The whale came to the surface _____ times. It spouted _____ times, with _____ seconds between spouts. Then it dived

for _____ minutes (or seconds) before spouting again.

Describe any colors, markings, scars, scratchmarks, brands, tags or deformities that you saw on the whale _____

_____

If you saw a tag, what color was it and where was it located on the whale (sketch) _____

Describe the whale's behavior (did it jump, make any noise, show its entire head, approach, flee, or ignore your boat, etc.) _____

_____

Describe any birds, fishes or other marine life associated with the whale _____

3. IDENTIFICATION

Field marks of most whale species from the Gulf of Maine are diagrammed below. Some features are difficult to see. Please circle any features that you saw. Sketch any additional observations in boxes marked "other." In order to avoid bias, our diagrams are not necessarily in any particular order. We will reply by mail to each sighting report received and will include a tentative identification of your whale. If you already know the name of your whale write it here _____ , then circle what you saw. Please remember that one piece of accurate data is far more useful than several pieces of questionable data.

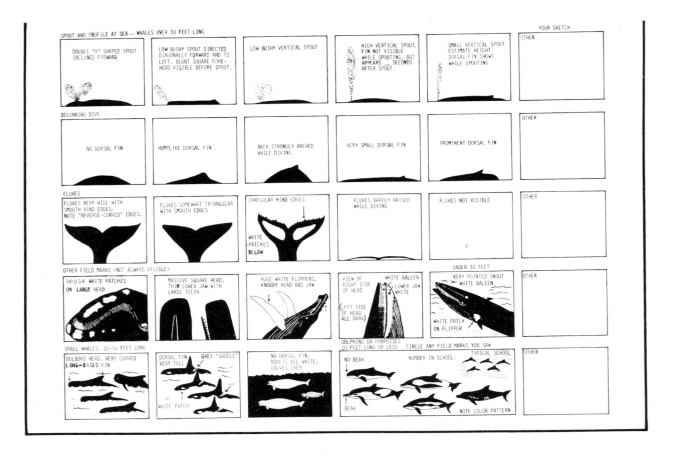

FURTHER READING

General:

Cousteau, J. and P. Diole. 1972. *The Whale: Mighty Monarch of the Sea.* New York, Doubleday and Co.

Hill, D.O. and R. Ellis, 1975. *Vanishing Giants.* New York, Rare Animal Relief Effort, c/o Audubon Society, 950 Third Ave., NY 10022.

MacIntyre, J. (ed.). 1974. *Mind in the Waters.* New York, Charles Scribners' Sons.

Matthews, L.H. (ed.). 1968. *The Whale.* New York, Simon and Schuster.

Nayman, J. 1973. *Whales, Dolphins and Man.* New York, Hamlyn Pub. Co.

Norris, K.S. 1974. *The Porpoise Watcher.* New York, W. W. Norton and Co., Inc.

Ommaney, F.D. 1971. *Lost Leviathan.* New York, Dodd, Mead and Co.

Seed, A. (ed.). 1971. *Toothed Whales.* Seattle, Pacific Search Books.

Seed, A. (ed.). 1972. *Baleen Whales.* Seattle, Pacific Search Books.

Wood, F.G. 1973. *Marine Mammals and Man.* New York, R. B. Luce, Inc.

Wray, P. 1974. *The Whale Book.* Boston, Endangered Species Productions, 84 Berkeley St.

Scientific:

Allen, G. M. 1916. *The Whalebone Whales of New England.* Memoirs of the Boston Society of Natural History, 8 (2):1-322.

Mitchell, E.D. 1973. *The Status of the World's Whales.* Nature Canada, 2(4):9-25.

Mitchell, E.D. (ed.). 1975. *Review of Biology and Fisheries for Smaller Cetaceans.* Journal of the Fisheries Research Board of Canada. Vol. 32, No. 7, 875-1242.

Nishiwaki, M. 1972. General biology, *in:* S.H. Ridgway (ed.). *Mammals of the Sea: Biology and Medicine.* Springfield, Illinois, Charles C. Thomas Pub., pp. 3-244.

Richardson, D., S.K. Katona and K. Darling. 1974. Marine mammals. Chap. 14 *in: A Socio-economic and Environmental Inventory of the North Atlantic Region, Sandy Hook to Bay of Fundy.* South Portland, Maine, TRIGOM (The Research Institute of the Gulf of Maine).

Schevill, W.E. (ed.). 1974. *The Whale Problem.* Harvard University Press, Cambridge, Mass.

Sergeant, D.E. 1961. *Whales and Dolphins of the Canadian East Coast.* Fisheries Research Board of Canada, Arctic Unit Circular 7.

Tomilin, A.G. 1957. *Mammals of the U.S.S.R. and Adjacent Countries,* Vol. 9, Cetacea. Israel Program for Scientific Translations. Available from the U.S. Department of Commerce, Clearinghouse for Federal Scientific and Technical Information, Springfield, Va., 22151.

immature gray seal on halftide ledge; blue hill bay, maine

INTRODUCTION

Seals and humans for centuries have held a mutual curiosity for each other. Seals often surface very near to boats, stare with their inquisitive globular eyes and then suddenly dive with an exuberant slap of the powerful rear flippers. For humans, however, seals have not been merely the object of study for the curious naturalist or scientist. For thousands of years seals have been hunted in the Arctic to provide life's essentials for natives and their dogs: meat, oil for light and heat, hides for boots, clothing and skin boat covering, and strong rawhide thongs for harnesses, lashings, and tools. However, the insatiable desire of white markets for furs made seal skins an important trading item. Small scale commercial sealing of the immense herds in the Canadian Arctic began in the seventeenth century. By the early nineteenth century seal harvesting was recognized as a lucrative industry and it compensated for the declining bowhead whale and sperm whale fisheries.

Intense hunting of harp, hooded, bearded and ringed seals and of walruses has severely reduced stocks and caused us to realize that survival of these species will depend on good management and protection efforts. Recent public awareness of wasteful exploitation and plundering of seals has stimulated population studies and scientific investigations to learn more about all aspects of seal biology. Moreover, the Marine Mammal Protection Act of 1972 provides a moratorium in U.S. waters on the taking, killing or harassing of all species of whales and seals as well as sea otters, polar bears, and manatees.

Wildlife observers on New England's coastal waters are fortunate that seals may be easily viewed basking and resting on numerous

harbor seal cow with nursing pup, typical seal ledges in background

D.D. Tyler

near-shore rocky and seaweed-covered ledges and small islands. Unlike whales which are often glimpsed only momentarily while surfacing to breathe, seals regularly rest in full view and provide the careful observer with plentiful opportunities to study the rearing of pups and the habits and interactions of young and adult seals on the rookeries or "haulout" ledges.

The best opportunities for successful viewing of seals exist along the shores of Maine from Kennebunk downeast to Machias. From almost any coastal village, patient inquiries of fishermen and residents and a well-planned row or paddle to a near-shore ledge on the low tide will provide a rewarding few hours of seal-watching. Or, preferably, one may take passage on a fishing boat or cruise boat to which seals have become accustomed. Attempts to approach a colony of seals undetected usually fail. However, a cautious approach, terminating at several hundred feet from the haulout ledge, will permit time for careful viewing with binoculars.

We hope that readers of this guide will find exhilaration in the wilderness experience of seal watching. Readers should become familiar with field marks to distinguish the harbor seal from the gray seal since both are commonly seen in the Gulf of Maine. Although sighting of a harp seal, hooded seal or walrus may be a "once in a lifetime" probability, it is hoped that every reader might be prepared to recognize one of these species on his excursions in New England waters.

The mammal order Pinnipedia, which includes seals, sea lions and walruses, consists of 31 species comprising three families: the earless or "true" seals of the north (Phocidae), the eared seals which include sea lions and fur seals (Otariidae), and the walruses (Odobenidae).

"True" seals use their rear flippers for power in swimming and cannot turn them forward for walking on land. They are often called "wrigglers" due to the hitching motion which they use to move about on their bellies. They have well-furred flippers with nails of similar size on all digits, mammaries with two or four teats, internal testes and no visible ex-

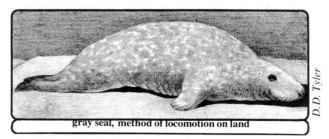

gray seal, method of locomotion on land

D.D. Tyler

ternal ear. True seals are found in marine, estuarine and fresh water environments. There are 17 species of true seals; 4 may be found in New England waters. Two species, the harbor seal and the gray seal, occur regularly in Maine waters and the harbor seal occurs seasonally in scattered numbers south to Long Island Sound. Two additional species of true seals, the hooded or bladder-nosed seal and the harp seals are common to eastern Canadian arctic and subarctic waters. Only rarely do individuals of these species stray south to New England waters.

Eared seals include the fur seals and sea lions. They use their forelimbs for swimming in water and can turn their hind limbs forward for walking on land. For this reason they are also called "land seals". Fore and hind flippers lack fur, have black palms and soles and flippers have reduced nails on outer digits. In addition, mammaries have four teats, testes are external, and these seals have a visible outer ear. Eared seals are found exclusively in salt water, but none of the 13 species occurs in New England or the North Atlantic.

Walrus share most of the characteristics cited above for the eared seals. However, they have lost the external ear, the tail is enclosed in a web of skin and the testes are internal. Walrus occur in the arctic sea and northernmost waters of the North Atlantic and North Pacific oceans.

All pinnipeds are highly evolved for aquatic life, but return to land or ice to bear young, mate, bask in the sun and to interact socially. All are exclusively flesh eaters and although feeding behavior and diet vary for each species, most seals adapt to items easily foraged near haulout ledges. Harbor seals prefer fish such as herring, alewives, and flatfish (flounder) but will also eat bony fish such as sculpin. Seals are also fond of squid. The walrus consumes clams, mussels and whelks. Small fish are caught and swallowed whole; however, you might view a harbor seal holding a larger fish in its flippers while stripping the flesh from the skeleton, which is discarded. Each day a seal consumes prey equivalent to about 6 to 10 percent of its body weight.

D.D. Tyler

harbor seal ripping mackerel apart

Compared to land mammals, all marine mammals evolved to large size, which is beneficial in a cold environment where a large body volume to surface ratio is important. The smallest pinniped is the ringed seal, weighing about 200 pounds and the largest is the southern elephant seal weighing about 8,000 pounds.

As you study the body form of a basking seal, note the streamlined, torpedo-shaped torso with limbs reduced and modified for swimming. In this respect seals demonstrate a more extreme evolution in anatomy than other water-loving carnivores such as the sea otter or polar bear. Modifications of the limbs and feet into flattened flippers has given the order its name Pinnipedia, which means feather-footed or winged-footed. Streamlining is enhanced by flattening the limbs against the body and by withdrawing external genitalia and mammaries beneath the smooth surface of the body. The skin is adapted to the water environment, having a thick, tough epidermis richly supplied with blood vessels and covered by flattened hairs which form two fur layers well supplied with large oil glands. Underlying the skin is a layer of blubber which acts as insulation against cold and as a source of reserve energy.

Blubber also provides buoyancy and padding to enhance the streamlined body shape.

Most pinnipeds gather in large groups (colonies) at traditional ledges, islands or ice packs (rookeries) at breeding time. Seal watchers of New England can best study breeding behavior of harbor seals in Maine from May through July. Mature females (cows) give birth to single young called pups. The tan or gray pups weigh about 25 pounds at birth but usually double their weight in about three weeks when they are weaned. Pups can swim immediately at birth but prefer to bask and nurse frequently on the ledges. Aggressive sparring between males and courtship and mating behavior may be observed in the water near ledges in early summer.

Like all other mammals, pinnipeds use lungs to breathe air in order to supply oxygen to body tissues. In humans, cessation of breathing and pressures associated with deep diving are formidable problems. However, all pinnipeds, like cetaceans, have remarkable diving capabilities. You will marvel at the ease with which seals surface, ventilate the lungs rapidly and again dive and remain submerged for periods of five to twenty minutes depending on their activity. Seals have been recorded at depths of over 475 feet. To withstand pressures at depth, the seal empties its lungs prior to diving, and depends on oxygen stored by the hemoglobin of the blood and myoglobin of the muscles. While submerged, blood circulation to most of the body is drastically curtailed, with the exception of the brain and vital internal organs. In addition, heartbeat slows to as low as one-tenth the normal rate, and body temperature and metabolic rate are lowered in order to conserve oxygen.

In addition to diving capabilities, some species of seals are known to emit underwater sounds to echolocate breathing holes in the ice or to help in the pursuit of prey for food. Pinnipeds have evolved a unique body form which allows them to perform their life functions with grace and agility even under harsh environmental conditions.

We hope users of this guide will be inspired to read about species of pinnipeds found in other regions as well as those briefly introduced here. A listing of suggested reading is given at the end of this section.

SUMMARY OF OCCURRENCE OF SEALS IN THE GULF OF MAINE

Family / *Species* / Common Name	Western North Atlantic Range and Distribution	Habitat	Estimated Abundance in Gulf of Maine	Relative Dominance in Gulf of Maine
Phocidae / *Phoca vitulina concolor* / Harbor seal	Labrador to Maine; scattered colonies to New York. Occasional strays to Carolinas	Inshore resident of bays and estuaries. Breeding, sunning, and resting on half-tide ledges	6000+ in Maine waters; 5000-6000 Canadian Maritime provinces	Common
Phocidae / *Halichoerus grypus* / Gray seal	Gulf of St. Lawrence to coast of Newfoundland; S. to Massachusetts. Dispersal outside of breeding season	Remote coastal ledges of Maine and sand shoals near Nantucket	18,000 in Maritime province waters; 100+ seasonally in Maine; breeding colony of 10-15 at Nantucket	Occasional in U.S. Gulf of Maine waters
Phocidae / *Pagophilus groenlandicus* / Harp seal	N. Atlantic and adjoining Arctic waters	Pelagic, breeding on pack ice: migratory	Occasional stray	Rare, accidental

Name	Range	Habitat	Abundance	Dominance
Phocidae *Cystophora cristata* Hooded seal	S. Greenland and Baffin Island to Gulf of St. Lawrence	Pelagic, breeds on drifting floe ice	Occasional stray	Rare, accidental
Odobenidae *Odobenus rosmarus rosmarus* Walrus	Ellesmere Island to Barrow Strait, S. to Hudson Bay and Hudson Strait	Remains in near-shore waters of remote islands or ice	Rare visitor	Rare, accidental

SPECIES ACCOUNTS, SEALS

John Quinn

approximate length:
male—6 feet, female—5 feet

HARBOR SEAL, COMMON SEAL
(*Phoca vitulina concolor*)

Harbor seals bask and rest on many near-shore half-tide ledges and small islands in bays, harbors and estuaries of the Gulf of Maine. This species shows curiosity for human activity near shore, and individuals often come quite close to boats during high tide foraging hours.

Adult males are about 6 feet long compared to about 5 feet for adult females. Maximum weight is about 250 pounds. Fur color varies greatly from light gray or tan to brown and red, irregularly spotted or blotched with black. Also, immatures and adults appear dark in color when wet, but can be very light when dry, particularly with a new coat following molting season in late summer.

The harbor seal head viewed in profile reveals a short muzzle and a concave (doglike) forehead. The eye is about equidistant from tip of nose to ear opening. Viewing the head from the front, the nostrils appear to form a broad V almost meeting at the bottom.

HARBOR SEALS

front view   side view   fur pattern

D.D. Tyler

The harbor seal is widely distributed on both sides of the North Atlantic and Pacific Oceans, adjoining seas, and even in landlocked lakes. It is a permanent resident in the Gulf of Maine but appears to be only a winter resident of bays south of Cape Cod. Its habits are closely tied to the tidal cycle. Day or night, individuals return to ledges on the early falling tide, where they haul out and rest in groups. During high tide, the seals disperse and hunt for food.

In spring, adults migrate into upper reaches of bays and estuaries. Pregnant females, mothers and pups stay on protected ledges apart from males and juveniles. Herds reassemble after pups are weaned in late June and July. In late fall colonies move to ledges in deeper water. Sunning on ledges is less frequent during winter months.

There are at least 6000 harbor seals in Maine waters, and 5000 to 6000 in the Canadian Maritimes including about 900 in the Canadian waters of the Bay of Fundy. Probably several hundred individuals occur in waters south of Maine. Harbor seals are well distributed along the Maine coast, with greatest concentrations occurring in lower Penobscot Bay, Machias Bay, and off Swans and Mount Desert Islands.

Storms, abandonment by the mother, disease, parasites, and possibly predation on young seals by sharks or killer whales kill about 20 percent of the population each year.

Mature males probably suffer yearly mortality close to 30 percent. Sexual maturity is reached at 3 to 5 years and full growth at about 10 years. Harbor seals have lived to be 35 years of age in captivity.

During the late 1800's, Maine offered a one dollar bounty on harbor seals in order to reduce the population and perhaps increase the amount of fish that could be caught by humans. By the early 1900's, Maine's harbor seals were nearly exterminated in certain localities with no noticeable affect on fish catches. The seals made a good comeback after the bounty was lifted. Until passage of the federal Marine Mammal Protection Act in 1972 seals were occasionally taken for use as mink food, for trial production of leather products such as climbing skins for skis and, more importantly, for use in biomedical research and for public display. The Protection Act permits taking of wild seals only by permit in U.S. waters.

GRAY SEAL, HORSEHEAD SEAL
(Halichoerus grypus)

This large seal occurs in eastern Maine waters in small numbers. Individuals usually mingle with Maine's harbor seals on sunning ledges during summer but mature bulls and cows apparently return to breeding areas in Canadian waters in the winter. Immature gray seals are difficult to distinguish from adult harbor seals, overall body size being similar. Adult males may reach 8 feet and up to 800 pounds. Adult females of this species are considerably smaller, only reaching about 7 feet and 550 pounds.

The most distinctive field mark is the "horsehead" or "Roman nose", which is more pronounced in males than in females. The nostrils are well separated, and look like a W when viewed from the front. The eye is located closer to the ear than to the nose.

approximate length:
male—9 feet, female—7 feet

The coat color of both sexes varies considerably. Females are often quite light-colored in the neck area but become darker to gray or brown on the back, with irregular spots and patches of black or dark brown on the lighter background. Males have light spots on a dark brown, black or gray background. The species name is not descriptive, since all seals found in the Gulf of Maine appear gray when wet.

The gray seal inhabits both sides of the North Atlantic with major populations in eastern Canada, Iceland, and northwestern Europe. The western Atlantic population is centered in the Gulf of St. Lawrence with a relatively large breeding center in the Northumberland Strait and breeding colonies near the Magdalen Islands, Basque Islands and Sable Island. The world population is about 100,000 with two-thirds of these in the British

GRAY SEAL

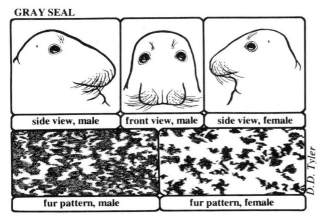

side view, male | front view, male | side view, female

fur pattern, male | fur pattern, female

D.D. Tyler

Isles and about 18,000 in the Canadian Maritimes. Somewhat fewer than 100 live in the Grand Manan archipelago of the Bay of Fundy. Probably fewer than 100 individuals occur in Maine waters during summer months. Most are yearlings and juveniles, which range widely after the breeding season. The southernmost gray seals occur on shoal islands near Nantucket and number 10 to 15 individuals.

Gray seals prefer exposed offshore rocky ledges. They have been sighted most often in the approaches to Mount Desert Island, Swans Island and lower Penobscot Bay.

The cream-white colored pups are born in February in Eastern Canada. Pups weigh 35 pounds and gain 4 pounds daily while nursing the mother's fat-rich milk. Pups begin molting within two weeks, retaining a light brown to gray coat. When about three weeks old, pups are weaned and remain on the breeding grounds until molting is complete.

Unlike harbor seals, mature gray seal bulls defend territories against intruding males, especially in crowded conditions. Males maintain harems of up to six cows and mating occurs on land and in water about two weeks after the birth of pups.

In crowded breeding grounds up to sixty percent of first year animals may die and up to forty percent of the adult males; however, calf mortality may be as low as ten percent per year when adults are well separated on the breeding grounds.

Gray seals have lived 41 years in captivity, but the oldest wild seal taken was a female of 34 years.

John Quinn

approximate length: 6 feet

HARP SEAL, GREENLAND SEAL, SADDLEBACK SEAL
(Pagophilus groenlandicus)

The beautiful harp seal, which gets its name from the dark harp-shaped or horseshoe-shaped pattern on the back, shoulders and flanks, is a rare visitor to the Gulf of Maine. It resembles the harbor seal in body proportions and head shape, but is considerably larger. Adults are about 6 feet long and weigh about 400 pounds. The pure white newborn pups weigh about 25 pounds and develop an irregularly spotted coat very similar to the harbor seal. Adults are light white, cream or tan with a series of dark blotches or solid

HARP SEAL

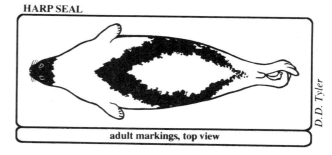

D.D. Tyler

adult markings, top view

patches forming the harp-shaped pattern, which is most pronounced in males.

The harp seal is found in the open seas of the North Atlantic and Arctic Oceans and north of Russia. Occasionally, individuals from eastern Canada or the Gulf of St. Lawrence stray south into the Gulf of Maine. Sightings of harp seals have been made in Penobscot Bay and Casco Bay, Maine and as far south as Cape Henry, Virginia. The incidence of strays is unknown, and no doubt is underestimated because few people are on the lookout for rare species and it is easy to confuse young harp seals with harbor seals.

Harp seals studied in eastern Canada have a complex annual cycle of migration and reproduction. In fall, scattered schools migrate from the Arctic to gather in two main herds: the "gulf herd" (Gulf of St. Lawrence), and the "front" herd (east of Newfoundland). During February and March the beautiful white-coated pups are born on the sea ice. Up to thirty-five million harp seals lived in northern seas two hundred years ago, but hunting of the pups for their fur has reduced that number by more than 90 percent. White-coat pups are clubbed and skinned on the ice, primarily by Norwegian and Canadian sealers. As a result of declining stocks and public pressure, harvesting of harp seals in the Gulf of St. Lawrence is restricted to landsmen arriving on the ice by small craft or snow machine. Strict quotas have been placed on seals to be taken on the ice off Newfoundland. Responsibility for management of the seal herds lies with the Fisheries Research Board of Canada and the International Commission of North Atlantic Fisheries (ICNAF).

The seal hunt takes place within about three to four weeks after pupping begins, before pups begin to molt their white coat and enter the water. After mating is completed in April to June, adults molt, either on ice or while at sea, and herds scatter and move north again.

Natural mortality is caused by storms and accidents amid drifting pack ice, abandonment, and predation on young by killer whales and sharks. Harp seals eat fish, primarily capelin, herring, cod and groundfish, as well as planktonic crustaceans such as shrimp.

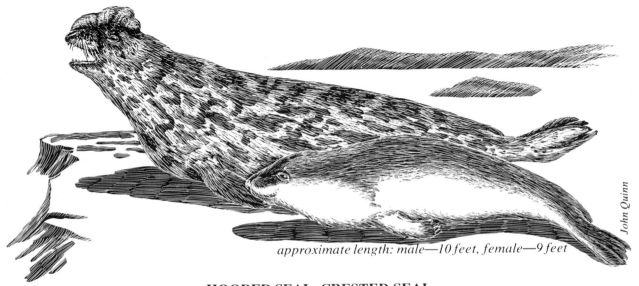

approximate length: male—10 feet, female—9 feet

John Quinn

HOODED SEAL, CRESTED SEAL
(Cystophora cristata)

Male hooded seals are up to 10 feet long and weigh up to 900 pounds. Males have a remarkable hood-like structure on top of the muzzle which can be inflated to form a crest almost twice the size of a football. In addition, males have an inflatable nasal membrane which can be blown through the nostril as a large balloon-like sac. Female hooded seals are slightly smaller than males and do not have a hood or nasal sac.

Adults have a distinctive bluish-gray coat which is spattered with dark, irregular spots.

The face, beginning just above the eyes, is solid black. The head is larger and the muzzle heavier than in the harbor seal, with a broader, more flattened nostril area when viewed from front. Pups are born from the end of March to

HOODED SEALS

side view, male	side view, female
crest inflated, male	nasal sac inflated, male

fur pattern

D.D. Tyler

the first part of April. They are about 3.6 feet long and 50 pounds in weight. Pups are called "bluebacks" because the exceptionally beautiful silver-gray coat of the back is sharply defined from the cream white fur of the undersides and belly.

The North Atlantic population of hooded seals numbers between 300,000-500,000 and is located mainly in the East ice from Bear Island and Spitzbergen to Jan Mayen, Iceland and Denmark Strait. Approximately 75,000 occur off southern Greenland and southeastern Labrador and about 1,000 occur in the Gulf of St. Lawrence. It is stragglers from these areas which occasionally reach the Gulf of Maine. A female and newborn blueback pup were photographed at North Harpswell, Maine in 1928 and another such pair were seen at South Brooksville, Maine in April, 1974. Hooded seals have been sighted several times south of Cape Cod and even at Cape Canaveral, Florida.

Hooded seals like deep water and prefer to bask or bear pups on large, drifting ice floes. Their migratory habits are poorly understood.

Hooded seals live a solitary life for most of the year, and are believed to favor monogamous reproductive behavior with bull, cow and pup associating closely during whelping in late March. Both adults fiercely defend their pup until it is weaned at 2-3 weeks of age.

Adults mate in April or early May and return to sea while pups remain on drifting ice floes for up to two more weeks before also taking to the sea.

Hooded seals feed on redfish, Greenland turbot, octopus, squid, herring, capelin, cod, shrimp and mussels.

WALRUS
(Odobenus rosmarus rosmarus)

The walrus is another very rare visitor to the Gulf of Maine. It is the largest member of the pinniped order and would not easily be mistaken for any other species. The walrus has a short squarish head with a moustache bearing several hundred yellowish sensory whiskers, each about 4 inches long, which aid in locating and grasping food organisms. The most distinguishing field mark for both sexes are the long tusks which grow continuously. The rough, wrinkled skin is up to 2.5 inches thick in a male's neck. The relatively sparse coat of reddish brown hair may be almost absent in older animals. The neck appears massive due, in part, to unique pouches which are part of the elastic pharynx and extend back laterally between the muscles of the neck. When inflat-

ed they can be used for buoyancy during sleep or if the animal is wounded. They are also used in sound production.

Adult males may reach 10 feet in length and 2000 pounds in weight. Females are smaller, about 8.5 feet long and 1250 pounds in weight. Walrus calves weigh about 120 pounds and are almost 4 feet long when born in April and early May. They are often seen clinging strongly to the mother's back. Calves nurse for over a year with no other source of food. Weaned calves may stay with the mother for a second year or more, perhaps because they have difficulty getting food until their tusks grow long. Tusks, which are really the elongated permanent canine teeth of the upper jaw, begin to form when the animal is about four months

approximate length: male—10 feet, female—8 feet

John Quinn

old, reaching one inch at one year, 4 inches at two years, and 11 inches at five years. Tusks have been known to reach 40 inches and 12 pounds.

The walrus occurs in arctic waters of both the Atlantic and Pacific. In eastern North America the walrus reaches the north coast of Ellsmere Island, west to Barrow Strait and south to Hudson Bay and Hudson Strait. In historic times walrus occurred as far south as the Gulf of St. Lawrence, Sable Island (a known breeding ground in historic times) and even to Massachusetts. Fossil records indicate that the walrus has been an occasional visitor to the Gulf of Maine. Remains of walrus bones have been recovered from the Penobscot Bay at Orrington, Maine; Blue Hill Bay, Maine, and from the Georges Bank. As recently as 1937 a live walrus was reported at Bear Cove, in southeast Nova Scotia.

The walrus favors a habitat of drifting sea ice floating above shallow water feeding areas. The Atlantic walrus migrates irregularly, and most individuals remain year-round in arctic areas but follow the melting ice edge north during warmer months.

There may be between 20,000 to 40,000 walrus in the eastern Canadian arctic. Humans and killer whales are the walrus' only significant predators, but polar bears occasionally attack young walrus. Injuries caused by shifting ice and accidental crushing of pups by adults on land are significant causes of calf mortality.

Walrus feed primarily on clams which they dig from shallow sand or gravel bottoms by means of a side to side shoveling motion of the tusks. The soft parts of mollusks are sucked or torn from the shell. Worms, whelks, sea cucumbers and polar cod are also eaten.

Walrus have been hunted for meat, oil, hides for rope, harnesses, whips and boat skins; ivory from tusks is prized for making carvings, tools, weapons, and for use in scrimshaw art. The Canadian and Siberian governments still allow hunting by license. No international management or protective regulations have been adopted for this species.

FIELD IDENTIFICATION SUMMARY: GULF OF MAINE SEALS

Common Name / *Species*	Male, Female Length, Nose to Tail		Maximum Weight Adults	Coat, Fur	Head
Harbor seal *Phoca vitulina*	M	5-6 ft.	250 lbs.	Highly variable; light gray or tan with brown or red. Irregularly spotted with black. Pups born with gray or tan fur	Short snout; forehead profile concave (dog-like). Eye about equidistant from tip of nose and ear. Nostrils form a broad V almost meeting at bottom
	F	4-5 ft.			
Gray seal *Halichoerus grypus*	M	9 ft.	800 lbs.	Variable; general rule is females light gray or brown background with dark patches; males dark brown, gray or black with light blotches. Pups born with embryonal white fur	Long snout with profile of forehead and snout straight or convex ("Roman nose"). Head donkey shaped ("horsehead"). Eye closer to ear than nose. Nostril slits form a W when viewed from the front. Female has a smaller head than male
	F	7 ft.	600 lbs.		

Name	Length		Weight	Coat	Head
Harp seal *Pagophilus groenlandicus*	M	6 ft.	400 lbs.	Newborn pups — ''white-coats''; juveniles irregularly spotted gray and tan similar to harbor seal; mature adults may have distinct dark harp or horseshoe pattern on back and flanks	Streamlined dog like muzzle similar to harbor seal. Head and face dark in color compared with neck
	F				
Hooded seal *Cystophora cristata*	M	9-10 ft.	900 lbs.	Newborn pups — ''bluebacks'' — have silver-bluish gray back with white belly; adults gray with distinct black patches of irregular shape; black muzzle and face	Larger and heavier muzzle than harbor seal with broader, more flattened nostril area when viewed from front. Crest or hood on top of head and muzzle of mature male. Inflatable nasal sac in male
	F	slightly smaller			
Walrus *Odobenus rosmarus rosmarus*	M	10 ft.	2000 lbs.	Rough wrinkled skin with very sparse reddish brown hair	Short squarish head with large white tusks and stiff whiskers (both sexes). Pharyngeal pouches in neck area
	F	8 ft.	1250 lbs.		

SAMPLE SEAL SIGHTING REPORT FORM

SEAL SIGHTING FORM

Date: _____19___   Time: _____A.M.___P.M.___

Weather: bright sun___; partly cloudy ___; mostly cloudy ___: overcast ___; other _____

_____

Estimate wind speed: ____mph

Estimate temperature: ____°F.

Estimate sea state: Heavy ___; moderate ___; calm ___; flat calm ___

What was the stage of the tide? _____

Observed from: Boat ___ Plane ___ Island ___Shore ___

Location (if an unnamed ledge, give nearest island or landmark) _____

_____

How many seals sighted: Harbor_____Gray _____

Total counts of pups ____; yearlings ____; juveniles____; adults ____

Were binoculars used:____

Estimate viewing distance_____ft.

Please describe markings, coloration or other identifying features of seals sighted. Was

there any behavior or activity which was interesting or unusual? _____

_____

_____

Please mail sightings to:

David Richardson   Steven Katona
Fisheries Research Station   or   College of the Atlantic
West Boothbay Harbor, Maine 04575   Bar Harbor, Maine 04609

FURTHER READING

General:

Backhouse, K.M. 1969. *Seals* (World of Animals Series). New York, Golden Press, 96pp.

Lockley, R.M. 1966. *Gray Seal, Common Seal: An Account of the Life Histories of British Seals.* London, Deutsch, 175pp.

Maxwell, G. 1967. *Seals of the World,* World Wildlife Series 2. Boston, Houghton Mifflin Co., 151pp.

Scheffer, V.B. 1970. *The Year of the Seal.* New York, Charles Scribners' Sons, 200pp.

Stuart, Frank. 1954. *A Seal's World.* New York, McGraw Hill, 223pp.

Scientific:

Harrison, R.H. (ed.). 1968. *The Behavior and Physiology of Pinnipeds.* New York, Appleton-Century Crofts.

King, J. E. 1964. *Seals of the World.* London, British Museum of Natural History, 154pp.

Richardson, D., S.K. Katona and K. Darling. 1974. Marine mammals. Chap. 14 *in: A Socio-economic and Environmental Inventory of the North Atlantic Region, Sandy Hook to Bay of Fundy.* South Portland, Maine, TRIGOM (The Research Institute of the Gulf of Maine).

Ridgway, S. H. (ed.). 1972. *Mammals of the Sea: Biology and Medicine.* Springfield, Ill., Charles C. Thomas Pub., 812pp.

Scheffer, V.B. 1958. *Seals, Sea Lions and Walruses; a Review of the Pinnipedia.* Stanford, California, Stanford University Press, 179pp; 32pl.

APPENDIX

APPENDIX

DERIVATIONS OF SPECIES NAMES
FOR WHALES AND SEALS IN THE GULF OF MAINE

Common Name *Latin Name*	Derivation	Translation
Toothed Whales:		
Harbor porpoise *Phocoena phocoena*	Gr. *phokaina*, porpoise	Porpoise. ''Porpoise'' probably comes from Fr. *porc poisson*, pig fish
Pothead *Globicephala melaena*	L. *globus*, a globe, ball + *cephal* from Gr. *kephale*, a head	Black, globe-shaped head. An old male looks as if he is carrying a pot upside down on its head. The British name ''pilot whale'' probably comes from the belief of Irish fishermen that these whales could lead them to schools of herring
White-sided dolphin *Lagenorhynchus acutus*	Gr. *lagenos*, a bottle + Gr. *rhynchos*, a beak or snout. L. *acutus*, sharp, pointed	Sharp bottle-shaped beak

Name	Derivation	Translation
White-beaked dolphin *Lagenorhynchus albirostris*	L. *albus*, white + L. *rostrum*, a bill or snout	White-snouted bottle-beaked dolphin
Saddleback dolphin *Delphinus delphis*	Gr. *delphis*, a dolphin	Dolphin
Killer whale *Orcinus orca*	L. *orca*, a kind of whale, the great killer	Killer whale
Bottlenose dolphin *Tursiops truncatus*	L. *tursio*, porpoise, L. *truncare*, to shorten	Shortened porpoise, perhaps referring to the short beak
Gray grampus *Grampus griseus*	*Grampus* from the English name + ML. *griseus*, gray	Gray grampus. "Grampus" is a corruption of Fr. *grand poisson*, big fish
Striped dolphin *Stenella coeruleoalba*	Gr. *steno*, short or narrow + L. *caeruleus*, dark-blue, + L. *alba*, white	Short blue-white dolphin

Name	Derivation	Translation
Beluga whale *Delphinapterus leucas*	Gr. *delphis*, a dolphin + *a*, without + Gr. *pteron*,, wing, fin. Gr. *leukos*, white	White finless dolphin
Sperm whale *Physeter catodon*	Gr. *physeter*, a blower. Gr. *kata*, downward, inferior + *odon* from Gr. *odontos*, tooth	A blowing whale, *catodon* referring to the fact that there is only one set of teeth in this whale, in the lower jaw. Early whalers thought that the liquid wax in the head was the whale's sperm
Pygmy sperm whale *Kogia breviceps*	NL. *kogia*, "a barbarous and un-meaning name." L. *brevis*, short, + NL. *ceps*, genitive of *cepitis* or head	Peculiar short-headed fellow. The genus name may be related to the word codger, meaning a queer or peculiar fellow.
Northern bottle-nose whale *Hyperoodon ampullatus*	Gr. *hyper*, extra, beyond, + Gr. *odontos*, tooth. L. *ampulla*, a round bottle	Refers to the whale's rounded melon which extends beyond the jaws in large males
True's beaked whale *Mesoplodon mirus*	Gr. *mesos*, middle, the half + *ploe* from Gr. *pleo* to sail, from *ploion* floating vessel + L. *mirus*, wonderful	Wonderful middle-sized floating vessel

Name	Derivation	Translation
Dense-beaked whale *Mesoplodon densirostris*	L. *densus*, dense, compact + L. *rostrum*, a bill or snout	Dense-beaked middle-sized floating vessel
Baleen Whales:		
Finback whale *Balaenoptera physalus*	L. *balaena*, a whale + Gr. *pteron*, wing, fin. Gr. *physalos*, a kind of whale	Fin whale
Minke whale *Balaenoptera acutorostrata*	L. *acutus*, sharp, pointed + *rostrum*, bill, snout	Sharp-snouted fin whale. A Norwegian whaler named Minkie was known for shooting under-sized whales. Any small whale was called Minkie's whale. Gradually the common name of this small whale degenerated to Minke
Humpback whale *Megaptera novaeangliae*	L. *mega*, large + Gr. *pteron*, wing. L. *novaeangliae*, New England	Large-winged whale of New England. The huge flippers look like wings

Name	Derivation	Translation
Right whale	Gr. *eu*, good, true, + L. *balaena*, a whale. L. *glacialis*, frozen	True whale, living in cold waters. The whale got its common name because it was the right whale to hunt. It was slow, floated when killed and contained a great deal of valuable oil and whalebone
Eubalaena glacialis		
Sei whale	L. *borealis*, northern	Northern fin whale. "Sei" is the Norwegian name for pollack, and this whale appears off the Norwegian coast each year at the time when pollack first appear
Balaenoptera borealis		
Blue whale	L. *musculus*, a muscle with possible play on L. *mus*, a mouse	Muscular fin whale
Balaenoptera musculus		
Seals:		
Harbor seal	Gr. *phoce*, a seal + L. *vitulus*, a calf	Sea calf, also known as sea dog
Phoca vitulina		
Gray seal	Gr. *halios*, of the sea + Gr. *choiros*, a pig. Gr. *gropos*, hook nosed	Hook nosed pig of the sea
Halichoerus grypus		

Name	Derivation	Translation
Harp seal *Pagophilus groenlandicus*	Gr. *pagos*, ice + Gr. *philos*, loving. Groenlandicus — geographical reference	Ice loving seal of Greenland
Hooded seal *Cystophora cristata*	Gr. *kostis*, a bladder + Gr. *phoros*, carrying, referring to the inflatable nasal appendage. L. *crista*, a crest, referring to the hood	Bladder carrying seal with crest or hood
Walrus *Odobenus rosmarus*	Gr. *odous*, tooth + Gr. *baino*, I walk; supposing use of the tusk in helping the animal to walk. Norwegian rossmaal or rossmaar derived from earlier Scandinavian words meaning "whale horse"	Whale-horse with walking tooth

gift from Amy Miller.